The Best
AUSTRALIAN POETRY
2003

The Best AUSTRALIAN POETRY 2003

Guest Editor
MARTIN DUWELL

General Editors
BRONWYN LEA
MARTIN DUWELL

UQP

First published 2003 by University of Queensland Press
Box 6042, St Lucia, Queensland 4067 Australia

www.uqp.uq.edu.au

Typeset by University of Queensland Press
Printed in Australia by McPherson's Printing Group

Distributed in the USA and Canada by
International Specialized Book Services, Inc.,
5824 N.E. Hassalo Street, Portland, Oregon 97213–3640

Sponsored by the Queensland Office
of Arts and Cultural Development.
Acknowledgment is made to Arts Queensland
for their financial support in
the preparation of this book.

Queensland
Government
Arts Queensland

This publication is proudly sponsored by
Art Galleries Schubert.

Cover painting by Michael Zavros, *Red Glow*, 2002
Oil on canvas, 50 x 70 cm
Private collection. Courtesy of the artist
and Art Galleries Schubert, Queensland.

Cataloguing in Publication Data
National Library of Australia

The best Australian poetry 2003.

   1. Australian poetry — 21st century — Collections. I.
Duwell, Martin, 1948–　. II. Lea, Bronwyn, 1969–　.

A821.4

ISBN 0 7022 3420 6

CONTENTS

Foreword by Bronwyn Lea   *vii*
Introduction by Martin Duwell   *xiii*

BRONWYN LEA

FOREWORD

The Best Australian Poetry 2003, the first in what we hope will be a long and vibrant series, is a selection of 40 of the best poems published in Australian literary journals and newspapers in the preceding year. Poetry in Australia is thriving. According to my somewhat shaky mathematics, in 2002 there were exactly 100 volumes of poetry published (that's one poetry book for every five novels) and 27 themed anthologies containing at least some poetry. Australian newspapers published almost 400 new poems (as well as reprinting some classics) and Australian literary journals published close to 1,800 poems. As the general editors for *The Best Australian Poetry* series, Martin Duwell and I hope that this anthology will direct readers to the poetry collections of the poets they enjoyed in this and future issues, as well as point to the literary journals that continue to publish high-quality poems.

We regret that we have not included poetry from Australian internet journals in this anthology. The decision to limit sources to the print media was based, for this year at least, on logistics, but it is possible that this might change in the future. In the meantime, I'd like to point to some websites worth looking at, including *Cordite*, *Divan*, *Stylus Poetry Journal*, and John Tranter's hugely popular *Jacket*, which brings into conversation poets and critics from around the world. Taking a different tack, Coral Hull's *Thylazine* continues to make a case for poetry and activism, as well as provide an Australian poet directory—to which I am indebted in the course of tracking down some of the poets included in this anthology. And then there's Jayne Fenton Keane's *Slamming the Sonnet* website, which makes the most of web technology by using audio and video files to flesh out poetry and breath a little life into the critically-declared "dead" author. Last time I logged on, Queensland poet Samuel Wagan Watson held his own in a cyberslam against Yeats, Plath and Bukowski.

2002, like any year, was a time of things living and things dying. Most significantly it saw the passing of three major poets, Dorothy Hewett, Ron Simpson and Gary Catalano. The former was always a flamboyant, larger than life figure in Australian poetry but one who showed that poetry could still embrace the big questions of public and private lives. Simpson and Catalano were quieter writers, and it might be said they belong to the tradition that imported some of the values of the visual arts—especially a concentration on line—into our poetry. At the institutional level, Robert Adamson and Juno Geme's Paperbark Press shut its doors after seventeen years of publishing some of Australia's finest poets. Shortly after, Ivor Indyk announced a new arm to his publishing house: the publication of literary works by individual authors under the Giramondo book imprint. Another birth worth noting is Ron Pretty's revival of *Poetry Australia*, in this incarnation entitled *Blue Dog: Australian Poetry*. In Pretty's editorial for the inaugural issue, he backs up contributing essayist Michael Sharkey's assessment of the impoverished state of poetry criticism in Australia and puts out a call for 'thoughtful pieces written about contemporary Australian poets and their work'. Which seems a good idea.

Given this discussion, then, it is no accident that we have decided to kick off the inaugural issue of *The Best Australian Poetry* with a guest editor who is not a poet, but a poetry critic. Martin Duwell brings to this volume his experience that comes from thirty-five years in poetry publishing and criticism, as well as a passion for poetry that rivals any poet's. Presented with the task of selecting only forty poems from over 2,000 possible poems, Duwell has created (without much fuss) a terrific collection of high-quality poems that is sure to impress dedicated readers of Australian poetry and newcomers alike. Duwell possesses that rare ability Sharkey calls for in his essay 'Reviewing Now': 'the ability of read widely, without prejudice', which struck me immediately when I read his compilation and noted the diversity of form, voice, style, and subject matter. Duwell has a critic's eye for quality, but also an anthologist's sensitivity as to how individual poems converse — how they confront, contradict, affirm, and question one another.

Which brings me to another matter. I began writing this foreword—then stopped for a long while—in October 2002. It was the time of the bombings in Bali. Which is to say, I wrote this within history, which is to date it. Many poems were born of this time, and like the thousands of 9/11 poems before them, Bali-bombing poems whizzed around the internet and clogged open-mic readings across the country. How many of these poems will survive remains to be seen—not many occasional poems do—but their existence illustrates Denise Levertov's assertion (quoting Heidegger interpreting Hölderlin) that to be human is to 'be a conversation'. Many it seems turn to the poem when their human need for dialogue, 'in concretions that are audible to others', overwhelms them.

Martin Duwell was born in Brighton (UK) in 1948. He emigrated to Australia in 1957, with his parents, under the ten pound assisted passage scheme. As a nine-year-old his passage was free and so, for better or worse, he cost Australia nothing. His parents settled in Bundaberg where he completed his schooling before attending the University of Queensland. His doctorate, from that institution, is a study of the influence of American poets on a number of Australian poets of the 1960s and 1970s. He edited the literary journal Makar for a number of years and, with friends, developed it into a press which published poetry until its closing in the early 1980s.

He has published widely on contemporary Australian poetry both as reviewer and essayist. He has published a collection of interviews with the poets included in Makar Press's *The New Australian Poetry*; two anthologies of Aboriginal song poetry—*The Honey-Ant Men's Love Song* and *Little Eva at Moonlight Creek*—with R.M.W. Dixon; a selected poems of John Blight; two editions of *The A.L.S. Guide to Australian Writers* (with Laurie Hergenhan, Carole Hetherington and Marianne Ehrhardt); a collection of essays *And What Books Do You Read? New Studies in Australian Literature* (edited with Irmtraud Petersson) and was one of the editors of *The Penguin New Literary History of Australia*.

He lives in Brisbane, has three now-adult children and has worked in the University of Queensland's School of English, Media Studies and Art History for thirty years. He is now a Senior Lecturer. His dominant intellectual interests, apart from poetry, are the Old Icelandic Family sagas and Sturlunga Saga (a contemporary compilation of mainly thirteenth century Icelandic history) as well as Persian language and classical literature. He has visited Iran and Iceland a number of times.

Martin Duwell

Introduction

As the first in what Bronwyn Lea and I hope will be a long and increasingly distinguished list of editors of this series of annual volumes, it falls to me both to make the first selection and to write the first introduction to that selection. Anthologies themselves, with that slightly twee derivation of the name from the Greek word for flower, can be underestimated phenomena. For most of us they, rather than books by individual authors, are the first place where we meet poems that become important to us throughout our lives. My life as a poetry-reader began with a secondary school anthology and I feel fairly confident that, nearly forty years later, I could list most of its contents.

Historically, anthologies have been the way in which poems, especially lyric poems, have survived. Unlike the more ambitious epics, with their strong narrative base, lyric poetry has a slight inbuilt ephemerality. We owe our knowledge of early Chinese, early Greek, medieval Scandinavian, pre-Islamic Arabic and innumerable other poetries to fortuitous anthologies. Of course the main threat in the past to the survival of lyric poems has been the vandalism of invaders. Today, the major threat is posed by exactly the opposite phenomenon. Because the continued existence of pretty well all text can be guaranteed (leaving aside such possibilities as an invasion of paper- and digital-text eating aliens) the volume of material poses the largest threat. So the function of the anthology has moved rather from a protective to a selective mode.

Although I have never edited an anthology of contemporary poems, as a critic I have compiled endless anthologies in my head—what might be called virtual anthologies. I think critics, especially those who are not poets as well, probably do this continually. The impetus may derive from the fact that although a reader can never change a poem, he or she can put the poem in a different context by surrounding it with different poems. The effect this has is quite striking: what looks a sentimental poem among other such poems looks decidedly humane and sensitive when surrounded by a clutch of hard-nosed poems and vice-versa. The aim of these virtual anthologies is not a selecting of the 'best'—whatever that might mean—but the construction of a group of works whose interaction is interesting in one way or another. You can, for example, make an anthology that you feel will represent the variety of things that is happening at any moment or you can construct one that shows how different literary modes are transformed into modern poems.

The brief of this anthology is to make a selection of what, as editor, I think the best poems published in papers and journals for 2002 were. It is an invitation to what I hope is an informed subjectivity rather than a detailed defence of notions of quality. I can describe my methods though I am less certain as to how well I can describe the results. The essential method, I suppose, is to school yourself to have complex and inclusive responses and then to make quick subjective decisions. You introduce yourself to the poem and, more importantly, give the poem a chance to speak to you—my students are always bemused by my extended set of metaphors for the act of reading. If you get on well enough to remember things about the poem after a few rereadings, spaced out over days, then you put the poem on your shortlist for later reflection. In the case of this anthology, that process produced a list of strong responses to about twenty poems and another list of about thirty. The only complicating factor in all this was the knowledge that a number of journals and newspapers would still be publishing poems late in the year while the editing is going on—it meant that all my initial choices had to have a slightly provisional air.

About the results of this, when structured alphabetically, I am not so sure. It must be a kind of imprint of my tastes and prejudices but it is probably better for other readers to work these out. I do notice, though, some obvious features. For example, I tolerate a wide range of kinds of poetry—probably a result of being a poetry editor rather than a poet. Reading in the literatures of the world teaches us that the house of poetry is a large one indeed, with many rooms some of which don't even seem like rooms to outsiders. One of the dangers of a tendency towards a kind of poetic 'essentialism'—the belief that real poetry is obvious to any reader and if they can't see it then it proves that they are just badly educated in poetry—is exactly that it runs the risk of closing off whole wings of the meandering mansion of poetry. So this anthology is one in which a wide variety of kinds of poem appear—none are ruled out of court before the process begins. (Though even I would be hard pressed to include a contemporary bush-ballad.)

I notice also that, though I don't have a preferred mode, I like the linguistically intense, as long as they are not mere rhetoric. I can see also that I like lists—the way poetry and good prose accommodates lists is a fascinating area. Lists interrupt the existing rhythms of the writing, partly by being serial but also by being structured in a different way—are they alphabetical? are they in ascending or descending order of importance? I also notice that I'm increasingly attracted by emotional statements in poetry (perhaps because poetry has always done this brilliantly or perhaps because readers always respond well to it). Of course sentimentality is a disaster but poems which court it and remain successful usually finish up meaning a lot to me. I can also see how much I like poems—like those by Geoff Page and Geoffrey Lehmann here—which are built out of individual, often disjunctive, blocks into a whole. It is one of the ways poetry can be mysterious because it challenges the reader to intuit the larger unity. Beautifully articulated, syntactically sinuous single statements are one of the things lyric poetry does well, but only one. I notice also that I retain a belief, despite last century's scepticism about language, that poetry can still have a 'capturing-in-words' quality and manage it reasonably well. So the result of this mixed list of preferences is a very varied anthology. Many of the poets, while happy to be included, will probably be alarmed at some of the poems that their poem is keeping company with. That seems to me to be wholly a good thing.

Accidents of timing and travel have resulting in my writing most of this introduction in, of all places, Iran—a country I love dearly but which, at the most generous estimate, operates culturally only in a parallel universe to Australia. A few days ago I attended a poetry reading in which members of the audience snuffled and suppressed tears and one man kissed the hair of a local poet. It is a different world and, rereading the poems I have selected, I am struck by how different they seem when read in a warm room on a snowy and wet Christmas eve in Hamedan—a modern city built around the ruins of the ancient Median capital of Ecbatana. Simple references to local Australian phenomena—plants and flowers, even Sydney's summer bushfires—conventional in a poem when read in Australia, seem luminously pregnant here.

A final point I need to make, not entirely irrelevant to this, is that I have included Bronwyn Lea's 'These Gifts' here, a poem which is immensely evocative of Brisbane at this time of year. Our initial plan was that, as one of the two general editors of this series, she would not have poems included. In retrospect this seems a graceless reward for a commitment to a long period as a general editor of what we both hope will be an important annual series of books. So I have pulled rank (while safely out of the country) and included her poem.

ROBERT ADAMSON

ELEGY

(for Arkie Deye Whiteley)

There's a fig tree, its black trunk shines in the rain;
a beach with small waves and a shark net;
music coming from a house, an exquisite guitar,
tonight there is nothing more bitter.

A white moon above the school yard,
resonating chords, fruit bats beating humid air—
seagulls slice open the body of a drowned rat
as the ebb exposes the objects of the moon's haul.

A light flickers, a newspaper floats under the jetty.
Doc Watson can sound like a gentle waterfall.
The road to Taronga Zoo is incandescent tonight.
This bitter news arrives on the tide in an empty boat.

The Sydney Morning Herald

JORDIE ALBISTON

APOSTROPHE

Poetry is our physician, and poetry will heal us.
No one believes that conceit anymore. Poetry
has got all too easy, the whore, and should be
punished as such. Let us cut out the shite and
consider its fate, tear down the tablet and replace
our faith with a full set of new, cheaper laws.
Poetry has much to answer for as we rant our
raves and weave our mandalas of sand; it leaves
overnight like a circus from town, treads over
its tracks, the whole thing, come morning, gone.

Poetry is our physician, and poetry will heal you.
If only it were so. Dragging our dirge from
clinic to clinic, you weep your sore epic and fit
your ten lines to the shape of a name on a form.
The word terminal is heard, but soon forgotten
as the small print fades and the meter announces
it now takes foreign coins only. You go too far
or not far enough, and remember too late the
gold rule: though the web of regret is finely
knit, only fools blames their holes on the wool.

Poetry is my physician, and poetry will heal me.
(Someone used to sing me that.) But it seems
all the words in all the world cannot doctor me
back this time. O, ring out, wild bells! Enter
my head! Take the blank stressed beeps of my
dead decalogue and unhinge my tongue, make it
well! Yes, visit my sickness, and minister your
mixture of blessings and curses, dear muse:
prescribes adjectives, alcohol, answer machine.
Save my ends from their mediocre means.

_____

Island

JOHN ALLISON

TOWARDS THE HORIZON

The health of the eye demands a horizon – EMERSON

In Swedish it is *synkrets*—
sight-circle. And the evidence of eyes
is that space is curved
and that the membrane of the sky
arches over us
and arcs around the blue silence at the edge
of vision.
There we find some sense of equilibrium,
poised between the lyric
lift and epic weight
of our existence and the world's.
Birds migrating in their lines and skeins
find it perfectly.
*The line of equality and that of the horizon
are the same*, said Leonardo
marking out the shape of it on paper.

We talk like this, turning
every thought into filaments
which thread the space between our words
until that silence

fills the lattice-work of light,
until that blue of distance comes up close
and pours itself into
the apertures that suddenly appear,
these openings from the world into a world
awakening—
your eyes are the horizon
and this side of them
nothing ever will be quite the same again.

Meanjin

JUDITH BEVERIDGE

WHISKY GRASS

Only this morning I felt anxiety's tufted leaves, and with no
scythe or sickle, I put my lips to a common roadside weed,
survivor in poorly drained soils, and blew: my tongue feeling
for the strange venation, the mid-rib ligule fringed with hairs,
until it returned the sting of whisky grass and the taste of
brown flowers. Over and over the same note matting itself
into the ground. Birds passing seeds back and forth, their
mouths, too, my tune of undoing. So many reasons to be
torn, pressed down to the seeping wound, or the salve. So
many reason why beauty can't square up all people in this
world and give them the insouciance of flowers. All morning
my mind gone to seed in margins, waste places; held back

by the understoreys of wire and milky latex of plants no-one
would give their lapsed acres for. So many reasons raising
themselves to the repeating power of our mouths. We pull
all kinds of things out of the ground; we cut off what we can
and paint it clean. We let birds pull songs through hedgework
whose tidiness we can't attend to, let alone afford. Beauty
likes its borders green. So many reasons, deeply-lobed,
bird-dispersed, as to why the pinkest pouch in a wayside
field turns thorned and thistle-wild; why these whiskered

shoots claim my mind; and why nothing looks greener
against the rain. Sure, these leaves by nightfall might be

shredded by birds foraging among dirt dumped over yellow,
defoliated stems; the sap taken by dreams, as every rhizome
is raked from the ground. I don't know. I work a tune around
a crowning blade and let it loosen another runner, testing
the future. The wild may never give up its gestures. Not while
beauty poises itself on the edge, trying to name the place it's
native to; a tongue twisting round each bearded stalk, listening
from the understorey for a flute-like sound, so many reasons
staking their season again. All morning anxiety's notes pour
through head-high grass. The sky turns and turns and lets
the wind in first, then rain, then light—a shiver of exhausted
leaves; perpetuals that always seem to come too soon.

Blue Dog: Australian Poetry

KEN BOLTON

A PROSPECT OF THE YOUNG KB AS A CRITIC

For a long time I stayed in bed very late – MARCEL PROUST

I remember with a kind of spiritual/intellectual
'wince' the boredom of the papers on Sunday. The comics.
The last page, if you still hoped
for some relief (it was, after all, 'the last page'), featured Val
(*Prince Valiant*), *Raddish, Laredo Crocket* & maybe
The Potts … (& some puzzles, Chucklers, that I never did).

Raddish I remember with some affection. Though did
I feel it then? Rarely. In it a couple—or a threesome?—
     engaged in intellectual
problems thought to typify their late-middle-aged,
     maybe
almost 'battler' status. There was no action in these comics—
& in this instance, invariable, the old lady, her hair worn
     (unlike Val
's) in a bun (Val sported, when I think about it, a curious
     Cleopatra cut), dried a dish or waved an admonishing
     finger—& hoped

or worried that—say—money, which she hoped

would arrive, *would arrive*—& pay their bills. The bloke,
       though he did

hardly anything (& nothing that didn't go wrong)—read
       the paper, bottled beer—or carried *his* device, a manly
       hammer—tightened a val-

ve that needed loosening—& while he talked over his
       shoulder she wiped up & talked back. (As fair to call this
       'intellectual'

as 'abstract', I think.) *Maybe it would happen*, maybe it wouldn't,
       whatever '*it*' was & one rarely knew. In these comics

long-foreshadowed action—maybe

because it took so long & was uneventful—like tension 'going
       away' rather than definitely ending—did not *seem* like action,
       & maybe

Raddish held some microscopic fascination—how I think of it
       now—because, in a pasture out the window he grazed,
       the 'wild' or trump card we hoped

might one day be played—in a rescue of narrativity, surreal
       but consequential. *Raddish*, the last of the comics

on this last page, took its name from the badly drawn,
       sway-backed horse—suspended *leit motif*, incendiary
       loose-cannon narrative device—available, should its
       creators feel (as I did)

the need for it. In fact weeks would go by in which we did not
       catch sight of the beast—& then we did—leading his
       contemplative (not to say intellectual)

life, truly a Life of Riley, munching, chewing, raising his tail.
        Was he their unconscious? their libido? The Potts' *id*?
        'Val',

Prince Valiant's flaxen-haired betrothed would say, 'Val,
stick it to me.' But she never did—though she admired him,
        as *I* never could, while he practised his archery,
        sharpened his sword, '*had moods*'. Was this maybe
muscular Christianity *avant la lettre*? or a puritan paganism? Val
        never promised the violently insurrectionary the way
        Raddish did, or even the intellectual
far-fetchedness & 'possibility' of the horse—who had a
        rumoured history as a one-time winner: hopes hoped
of him had some basis. Val on the other hand, had done
        nothing—textbook stuff, dutifully, textbook battles,
        textbook dispensing of justice, textbook falconry. There
        was no melodrama. Val did
everything in orderly fashion. He would never even grow
        bored with himself, bored enough to come bursting
        through the door, cigar in his mouth, gun in
        improbable hoof, announcing, *He-haww! The Drinks are
        on me*, as the horse would … or would in the comics

I desired. *Was* the strip named after the horse, as I imagined?
        Then who were The Potts? Or *Wally & the Major?* Why,
        of the comics
on the other page, was the one I understood least the most
        intriguing—the modern one, temporal miles from Val

but geographic miles from me (I assumed it was America,
    though almost *too* literate—which made it, then,
    socio-economic miles from me, too)? where what they did
was *sit*, & amble around, in an airy open-planned lounge or
    den—& maybe
read the comix, or Sundays papers or a magazine. The heroine
    hoped
she would not be bored, & father—handsome, quizzical,
    sporty dresser—made dry remarks—as did mom
    (another intellectual)?

The young girl (eighteen? twenty-two?) wore Prince Val's
    hairdo, better than Val did,
& toreador pants & maybe lounged on her spine, oblique &
    petulant—& hoped
her boredom would end: like me she hated the comics … &
    Sundays … an attractive young *bourgeoise*—while I
    remained, *like Raddish before me*, a 'dark horse'—yet, like
    the girl, soon to grow *fiercely intellectual*.

———————
Heat

PETER BOYLE

NEARNESS

(for Margie)

The whirlwind that rose out of the book
filled the house.
The small woman with the dark hair
stood still, spinning in the open doorway.
Chestnut leaves circled the empty table.
I wanted to find my own road
but you had gone off with the roads,
you who I did not understand.
Someone dripping light from the curve of a low cloud
appeared in the waiting darkness.
Heavy and delicate, her eyes
hung silent in her head
and it was you—
as when suddenly passion clicks
and you know the words you have forgotten.

The vast house has too many doorways
to let the living monopolise it.
Or maybe it's only in the hour
when suicide drops away
that you discover death—

how it grows into your hands
whether you will it or not.

Darkness had passed over us both
and you cried out and entered the sky
while others failed to recognise their own death
and went on walking the same streets
never missing their shadows.
At that time we had just begun to hear the rumour
of a practice that would leave the body standing free,
the sky filtered through our locked fingers
and the earth spinning a little to one side.

Desire is the return of sunlight
as a wholly hidden language against the chill wall
able to let the paintwork shine.
Desire is the difficult treatise written by each breath,
the small book growing in the untranslated sun.

Island

GARY CATALANO

ARLES

(For Mary Hewitt)

Half the charm of visiting
a historied landscape
is to feel one can travel
back and forth, in time, at will.

Undeterred by the absence
of spuds and tomatoes
and having momentarily overlooked
the heart-stopping rate

of infant mortality,
today I'm living in Roman times
and am just about to make
my daily obeisance

to the civic gods,
who have blessed this city
and brought it peace. Tomorrow,
I daresay, I'll be back among

my own kind—those gawking
beer-swilling tourists
who go gaga over
soap-sized discs of goat cheese

in the streetmarket,
and who, on leaving Arles,
will remember that here they tasted
their first wafer-thin pizza—

but right now I just want
to take a bath with my friends
and visit the theatre
or the arena

and contemplate, if time permits,
the changes that have been made
since those hopeless Ligurians
squatted here in the mud.

The Age

JENNIFER COMPTON

CASTLE

O forgive me but I forget my name.
It was a long time ago when the men
came on horseback with their swords drawn.

I was a boy, not a man.
There were plenty like me.
We did what we were told to do.

It might be to carry a plate of food
up into the light of the hall
where the people were.

And then that day—I was underground—
I heard the noise and went upstairs
to see all the people killed.

The men—on horses—O
white and black and bay—drinking blood.
Nothing to do with me.

I sat all night on the bottom stair. I was cold.
And nothing stirred. Everybody dead.
At dawn I realised they had killed me.

I stood up and walked away from the castle.
As I walked across the meadow towards you
the ones like me were waking from their sleep.

Quadrant

M.T.C. CRONIN

THE FLOWER, THE THING

(for Greg McLaren)

Urgently, now, before us, the flower, the thing,
entered before any window would allow it,
always living, always posthumous, breached
by the world and unabstracted. Give luck
to your eye if you see it, miracle to your nose
if you smell it, and the completion to your skin
rubbing the sunset into the flower's hydris sea.
Don't be afraid of looking for the word which
will describe this perfectly for with the help
of the body the world will rise up, catch the wind,
and float to the clear surface of the waiting water.
Do you recall the world? Place your hand
on the place where it was cut from you and you
will know what pushes us to leave meaning.
Do we think, adrift, we will forget or be forgotten?
The flower answers that the mood has decided
its method of flying, its rest. The flower says
I have believed enormously, have you? And so,
the vulture, the hat, the hand, the cobra, the dog,
the sand, the arm, the trail, the reed, the two reeds,
the foot, the bone, the leaving, the basket, the back,

the folded cloth, the jar, the stand, the gold, the rope,
the tether, the sound, the viper with horns and the
sound of these like pins in the throat which are eased
by water ... and always now, before us, *the thing* ...

———————
Heat

STEPHEN EDGAR

EIGHTH HEAVEN

I open the flyscreen door and slip inside,
Easing it shut. Low voices—the radio?—
Drift from the dining room, although their words

Are indistinct. A milky sort of light
Clings to the ceiling, showing that the summer
Is well established here and the inner shadows,

However cool they may appear, are tacky
As bare thighs on a vinyl chair.
My mother, at the kitchen bench, is pouring

Afternoon tea, or would be, but I see
That, unsurprisingly, that red-brown ribbon
Is stationary and the steam hangs still,

A Lilliputian fog. Can time have stopped
So simply, in this simple suburb, at
This hour of day? And yet the radio

Is lit up and those voices natter on,
Talking the timeless issues of the day
And advertising their predated products.

The sideboard stands, as ever, well equipped
With seldom used utensils, special service:
The special teapot of white china, capped

With shining metal like a soldier's casque;
The little glasses with their Chinese figures—
Sum Fun Tu, Me Fun Tu, Tu Yung Tu…; plates

Of many colours with their hidden names,
Remembering far better than I can
Their few occasions. And there is my father

Standing in the lounge room, half-turned away.
I summon up some greeting and can feel
The words unbodied, though not a sound disturbs

The house's depth. I walk in and am baffled
To find, however much I move about him,
That that one aspect is still turned to me.

Unmoving, a one-sided hologram.
Net curtains billow at the window, frozen
In air, as though a child were crouched in them.

In the middle of the wall the oval mirror
Declines to represent me, though I come
So close my breath appears on it. I place

My right hand's fingertips against the glass
And feel the surface tension of a pool
Resisting, then reluctantly giving in.

My fingers come away with silvered ends
Which, as they sway, show scraps of furniture
And carpet, flowers in a vase.

Now I am gazing out across the park.
The afternoon is caught among the leaves,
Detained indefinitely out there, and in

My throat. My fingers are still wet from touching
The glass; I must have brushed them on my cheek.
At the back gate I see that I am leaving:

That is my arm there sliding the bolt shut.
A bowl of fruit is on a table by
A window. On the round face of the apple

Surmounting it is held the light of the world.
It sits there like a globe of crystal, or
A painted droplet—the Earth that Dante saw

When he looked down at last from the eighth heaven.
Within it, sworn to secrecy, flamboyant,
Swim all the ages and the hours.

Famous Reporter

MICHAEL FARRELL

SYDNEY

sydneys real as romance really is
centre of the wholesale fun trade
open your eyes to the heat like
smiling at illusions of riding pink
its nice to fizz but not to fizz out
here we pay a lot of attention to
collars the bluer the more we like it
pressed a far cry from the jewel of
the east & the fat fu beau with the
mumu unaccustomed clerics see aught
but fire which image is ever a com
fort sitting in cafes on at perfume
bottles the bush purely academic
rwing cats call it mice city undisturbed
civic pride gives awful calm to rivals
yet if the new york skyline holds
& jd salinger then sydneys the
ultimate in bridging voids &
bringing the universe to itself the
atmosphere of reality mountains in
that desired chunky accessibility

Philip Hammial

EVERLASTINGNESS

Caught on the crossing, undone
on the Ponte Vecchio. And thus, suddenly
in situ, the Everlastingness in which, by a series
of strange coincidences, we'd come to be involved
went by the way, a dissolve to a frame of coy
decoys afloat in the *cream* of society, its promise of rags
to riches forgotten the moment Dr. Kirov crawled
into the party on his hands & knees, tuxedo ripped
to shreds, 'Attacked', he gasped, 'by Tibetan.
bandits!' Frightened away, 1898, by Alexandra
David-Neel's wrathful goddess impersonation, they fell
on him, an envoy from the Czar who knew nothing
of the local religion & was proud of it, his grand
doggie style entrance perfect for this late 60s party
about to evolve to a higher plane, tantric, left-
handed, A.K.A. *free love*, its adherents impervious
to bullets, rubber or real, even those that explode
on impact simply another instance of Cosmic
Hallelujah for those with the wherewithal
to see them for what they were/are, today, three
more Hezbollah on their way to Paradise thanks
to Israeli sharpshooters, a read-along ball bouncing
against the Wailing Wall—CALLISTHENICS

FOR MARTYRS—those wasted limbs obviously
in need of some exercise. A real job, humping stones
from a quarry say, would do them a world of good. Work
makes you free, etc. I.G. Farben still thriving as Farbwerke
Hoechst, etc., a company that provides a caring environment
for its highly-skilled, well paid employees, etc., the caved-in.
V-2 launching sites in the Harz Mountains a sanctuary now
for a few losers filling their veins with diluted heroin. No
wonder their sugar plum visions have mutated to Chod-
like rituals—boiled *in situ*, in your own juice, broth
ladled out to your worst enemy as the jewelers
on the Vecchio wait, silver cups at the ready (glancing
now at the knick-knack shelf above my desk where
a miniature set of silver filigree furniture gathers dust,
a gift to my mother from a trip to Florence in '58) for
their share of the Everlastingness in which, by a strange series
of coincidences, we'd come to be involved.

Southerly

JENNIFER HARRISON

FUNAMBULIST

Coins fill the busker's hat
and, it's true, a thief will steal from the blind.
Satellites spin delicate journeys
in the woods above, space

in the guest room we never had.
Malleable, down below,
in the mute neon between streets,
we've touched only the details of maps.

Believing ourselves beamed upon,
we script new mercy themes
and here are the things I carry:
a silver bell, a desk, a lock of hair

some laurel flowers, a lantern
a *bonbonnière*, three scarves
a black cat, a peacock, a box of rain
a streak of lightning

a ladder, a pipe, a coffin, a fan
a pumpkin, a skull, a book of law.
Believing myself beamed upon
I carry one clap of thunder, some shrimps

and a globe, a bag of nails, a carton of crème
a roly-poly of doves.
I carry the city, the cleft mirror
the faked fight of the fist on the drum.

Blue Dog: Australian Poetry

MIKE HEALD

FIRE

Two percent more oxygen and you could never
be cajoled back inside the bush's myriad vessels:
you would inherit the air and all its creatures.
As it is you're muttering and glaring all season
as we tinker with our weapons and refine
our strategies of containment for when you rise
like a superman between the gods and us,
crumpling everything in your way, devouring
with just your breath. Yet even your ferocity
can't unsettle the core promises of order
like that other incautiously unearthed,
unearthly heat, the smouldering
from our formative conflagration,
and nature here tolerates your frenzy,
gearing your wayward brawn to a delicate
leverage to prise open dormant generations.

Some say you're the capable half of a tag-team
with those whose own capacity for mischief
will never be enough; or the rampant ecstasy
of those for whom your maelstrom of withering
embraces is fulfilment. Like your golds and scarlets
they're half-truths: throughout those first searing

imperial summers, you never dared to enter
the pristine forest, all massive columns
and broad chambers then: as those whose eye
remains steady in the havoc and can read
the warped languages of aftermath
have been repeating down the oblivious generations,
it's the crowded, scrawny crop we mow
the forest into, and the hasty, careless harvest,
that invites and feeds your ruinous appetite,
that inflates your achievements to disaster.

Salt

Clive James

OCCUPATION: HOUSEWIFE

Advertisements asked 'Which twin has the Toni?'
Our mothers were supposed to be non-plussed.
Dense paragraphs of technical baloney
Explained the close resemblance of the phoney
To the Expensive Perm. It worked on trust.

The barber tried to tell me the same sheila
With the same Expensive Perm was pictured twice.
He said the Toni treatment was paint-sealer
Re-bottled by a second-hand car dealer
And did to hair what strychnine did to mice.

Our mothers all survived, but not the perms.
Two hours at most the Toni bobbed and dazzled
Before the waves were back on level terms,
Limp as the spear-points of the household germs
An avalanche of Vim left looking frazzled.

Another false economy, home brew
Seethed after nightfall in the laundry copper.
Bought on the sly, the hops were left to stew
Into a mulch that grunted as it grew.
You had to sample it with an eye-dropper,

Not stir it with a stick as one mum did.
She piled housebricks on top, thinking the gas
Would have nowhere to go. Lucky she hid
Inside the house. The copper blew its lid
Like Krakatoa to emit a mass

Of foam. The laundry window bulged and broke.
The prodigy invaded the back yard.
Spreading across the lawn like evil smoke
It murdered her hydrangeas at a stroke
And long before the dawn it had set hard.

On a world scale, one hardly needs to note,
Those Aussie battlers barely had a taste
Of deprivation. Reeling from the boat
Came reffo women who had eaten goat
Only on feast days. Still, it is the waste

I think of, the long years without our men,
And only the Yanks to offer luxuries
At a price no decent woman thought of then
As one she could afford, waiting for when
The Man Himself came back from Overseas.

And then I think of those whose men did not:
My mother one of them. She who had kept
Herself for him for so long, and for what?
To creep, when I had splinters, to my cot
With tweezers and a needle while I slept?

Now comes the time I fly to sit with her
Where she lies waiting, to what end we know.
We trade our stories of the way things were,
The home brew and the perm like rabbit fur.
How sad, she says, the heart is last to go.

The heart, the heart. I still can hear it break.
She asked for nothing except his return.
To pay so great a debt, what does it take?
My books, degrees, the money that I make?
Proud of a son who never seems to learn,

She can't forget I lost my good pen-knife.
Those memories of waste do not grow dim
When you, for Occupation, write: Housewife.
Out of this world, God grant them both the life
She gave me and I had instead of him.

Australian Book Review

JUDY JOHNSON

SELF PITY

(from 'The African Spider Cures')

Have your jaw wired by a qualified surgeon at the Malago
    hospital
in Kampala, then wake from twilight sedation to hear the
    post-Amin

cellophane crackle of Radio Sanyu playing 'Back in the USSR'.
Relish the smells: the decadence of ether still squatting in your
    hair,
the pine-o-cleaned bedpan's faux-forest afterglow.

Accept with demure passivity the pureed maize meal and rice
which you must suck, with considerable effort, through a straw.

Stare at the Masai girl, in the opposite mosquito-netted bed
who was attacked by a hyena and now has no lips, cheeks or
    roof
of her mouth, but considerately covers what's left of her face

with the vista of zebras galloping the Savannah
on the teatowel the nurses have made her a veil from.

Feel better about your predicament. To reinforce this
sense of privilege, become aware
of the rugged-up stares of other patients (the ceiling fan
whacks their eyes with its beater)…The boy
whose Karimijong father spits green wads of tobacco across

the chequered floor and hunkers down by the bedside
on a two-legged chair. And the tracheotomy girl
from the Rift Valley who swallowed a stone and now

holds a finger to the hole in her throat
when she sings, Dalek-like, along with the radio.
View the chiaroscuro pre-storm light through the window
        ducking
and weaving, the sun's snail trail pulled around the
        whitewashed angles
of buildings. With dusk and the storm closing in, feel the
        growling in your belly

triggered by a moth flying over your bed. Salivate
at all dark green vibrations. Impress yourself.

Take on the name of the Wolf. Maximise your potential for
        intimidation
by wheeling your bed over to where the encroaching grey
        makes
your crouched figure grow long limbed and sinister-twitchy

as a character in the shadow-puppet theatre.
For the next step, you must practise bulimia's internal
gymnastics.

Draw digestive juices up from you stomach. Get used to the
taste
of your own bile, bitter and alkaline-soda as the waters of Lake
Tanzania.
Now choose the victim you most want to devour. It's time to
admit

you did not come to this cure to relive your self pity, merely to
indulge it.
Therefore, collect a gourd of cow's urine early in the dew-frost
morning,

then leave it stand until a clear film forms on top.
If this proves too difficult, the stainless steel sterilising urn
that exhales steam in the nurses quarters will do. And if not
the urn, then a mirror. Observe the small animal you have been
approaching with this toxin, sanguinely, and without lust, for
years.

Watch it twist and turn inside the silk it's rolled in, stuck to
what you are determined it will neither die of, nor escape from
while ever you are so dexterous at weaving discontent.

The Courier-Mail

AILEEN KELLY

THE WHIRLPOOL

Bones within my fingers grip
the cold compass-head and wrench
it round. The pole-pulled iron
reads south on its card but still asserts
entrenched within its body
an unarguable north in which
sometime out of County Cork
my father's father made port in
Southampton, my father sailed the wars
of his youth and found Winchester and I
walked St Cross and Selbourne building
my mind's map and then slapped myself
down on the backside of earth, where the inner
compass spins across its own backwards shadow
and each new tree or wall harbours strange birds.
In no-light at 3am the pedestrian memory
sketches all these journeys black on ghostwhite
and the map finds a new starting point,
an arrow labelled You
Are Not Here.

The tic of ear and eye-corner on pillow
locate the head, the head locates the body.

By such clues one continues
to navigate the physical, touching
finger to the other wrist, finding
the hard tender mound between itch and clot and scar
where a mosquito spiked under a bruise,
plucking the spine's tension, tracing length
by the hip cramped with long lying.
Thus one maps the body
of treacherous islands and cyclone waters
without reference to compass.
Turning slowly to the right there is
comfort giving oneself to the turn
and this whirlpool becomes the easiest
of navigations, where the water
has its own purpose.
Then magpie and butcherbird
bring too much dawn for black and white
and the morning is rosellas.

Blue Dog: Australian Poetry

JOHN KINSELLA

LYRICAL UNIFICATION IN GAMBIER

(i)
What remains barely the weather
report: sentencing labours of history
against all the beginnings, the maples
leafless, the houses barely porous.

(ii)
I ride roads I am not familiar with,
a figure of speech, chrome strips
between windows. To the south,
burial mounds. Resolution
deep and simpatico. Northwards:
the lake effect, the snow plough.

(iii)
Deer go down to bow and gun,
roadkill is a 'cull': beauty
in the eye of rhetoric
keeps the engine
ticking over.

(iv)
Cornstalks like rotted Ceres'
thin black teeth. To end with this.
A season of political arrangements,
remnant snow quarried
like that pitiless ocean.

(v)
The driver must resist
all beauty, the smell
of an unfamiliar passenger.
A door rattles, the car
is almost new. It is shut
properly. Speed limit.
Farm machinery. A (solitary)
white field enclosed
by thawed pages.

(vi)
Maples, oak … all kinds.
A tornado ripped through here
three months ago and didn't
touch the houses either side.
Birds warble in the engine
cavity. A cord of wood

stretches out below
the kitchen window.
He says we listen
differently.

Australian Book Review

Bronwyn Lea

THESE GIFTS

Days like these—cool afternoons
in late summer, a rain so delicate
you can sit in the backyard and let the mist
drizzle your face. There's no grass,
of course. A late heat wave has bleached
the lawn, burnt off the last of the tree ferns.
Just last week, children and the elderly
were suffering from heatstroke. Yet
these gifts that arrive late season—
an apology you hadn't dared hope for,
a rush of poems, an impromptu patience
with the world. You rest your head
against a silky oak, and by your cheek
two butterflies coupled in flight
sex it up. And the day has charmed you
with ephemera before you can object.

Heat

GEOFFREY LEHMANN

FATHER AND SONS

I

He's been away for a week,
so I telephone.
'Dad, your voice is too loud.'

II

Two weeks with my sister-in-law
and her ordered parenting:
my boys are like polished silver.

III

As I wash his dirty feet in the bath
his toes curl coquettishly.

IV

The cap still on the lens
he points his new red telescope.
'I can see the craters on the moon!'

V

Between courses my two boys
leave the Peking Inn
for a yoyo break.

VI

Hiding in a distant room
crying under a bed
sobbing to himself in gasps
I can't see him in the twilight.
'I was cleaning the car as he said,
but he kept on at me, finding fault.
It's always like this.
He doesn't want to pay me the money.'

VII

Your flight aims toward Delhi at midnight.
Brown eyes gaze up, his arms reach up
and draw me down, planting a chaste kiss on my lips.
Then he says: 'And good night mum, wherever you are.'
Next morning
taking his school bags from my car
face blank as a wall, he doesn't say goodbye.

VIII

'There are eighty seven different vegetables in this shop
and you'll eat only three.
How boring to be your father.'

IX

Looking for a poem to read
at school assembly,

my ten year old packs in his school bag
Frank O'Hara's 'Lunch Poems'.

X
'Good night, Mr Bubby,' I say.
'Bubby,' he says
testing the word doubtfully—a pet name or an insult.
Years later, aged 14, he still wants to be tucked up
and a good night kiss.
He smiles: 'Good night, Mr Lovely One.'
'That's what I was just about to say,' I say.

XI
The teenager's unblinking gaze: 'Dad,
you're too kind to be any good as a lawyer.'

XII
I pick up a beetle struggling in illuminated water
and launch it at some bushes.
Both taller than me now, we swim at night
in the blue glass mosaic pool
(affordable only at the end of their childhood—
inhabited by childish shouts and screams
for just two or three summers).
The heater's on and steam rises from the surface.
As we swim lengths

the underwater pool light refracts through wobbling liquid
and a ghost light bobs in distant eucalypts.
I stand at the shallow end
watching a large aircraft fly over, red lights blinking,
as young baritone voices
call out my given name.

Quadrant

EMMA LEW

THE CLOVER SEED HEX

Once my foot was like a cube of sugar.
I ran deep in the village, playing on a drum,
happy even with the stones on the road.
I swept the air like this with my hand.
Like a dove, but my father was behind me.

The one I took was a poor man, the one
who limped, and it turned out badly.
It is said that a married man and a woman
must be like a tomb. There was a stranger
who followed me home also. He put
his eye to the keyhole and looked at me.
He was a man already. I didn't see him.
I turned the water jug over on its mouth.

Men are never afraid. They know everything,
not like women, and in other ways
we have taken their hardness. A woman
has to be fine and weak. He loves her tears.
One man came close to me after a time,
and during the small feast I answered, 'Yes'.
Childlessness can come of dishonour.
In other words, mine was a black deed.

The mothers of the boys are passing
on the opposite side of the street,
the Nile side. They say, 'So and so
was ruined because of her'. Let them
talk and pass. I walk in fields
I am unfamiliar with, and it may be that
when I fall down I am under some spell.
In any case, half of beauty is darkness.
Are these things in our hands?

Island

JENNIFER MAIDEN

MISSING ELVIS

I. MISSING ELVIS AND TWO NAKED WOMEN AT THE LUDDENHAM SHOW

Last year, the Luddenham Show had Elvis
and two dancing girls in G strings. This
year, it's two blokes with beards who sing
like social workers. No Elvis. The crowd
watch patiently, applaud, join in:
perhaps still miss 'Suspicious Minds', but
there are compensations: real cream
on strawberries and pavlova at
a new stall, no thunderstorm
to spoil the fireworks. The fireworks,
as usual, are fine. No bridge
weeps brilliant Niagaras to the tunes
of recent pop nostalgia, just
something like a sudden flowerbed,
no music but thrilled children and
adults who need to explain it all
                           aloud, as if
to seem responsible for universal
processes of combustion, as if

responsibility is celebration. Elvis
had glitz and rhythm, was suited
to the fireworks. The Texan
columnist Molly Ivins graded
politicians on an Elvis Scale. What,
I wondered, would George W. Bush
rate on it?, as I shook the grit
of the showground from my sandals.
George of the Lethal Injection.
There is something Elvis-like
in winsome, dyslectic mumbles, but
his vocal tone is better than
his father's: not so prim,
so childlike and super-ego ridden.
W.'s nose is sharper, looks
more deadly than Senior's, like a beak
built to tear not peck, his mouth
a drier, twitchier line. Baghdad
is already bombed again. The fireworks
always seem louder since the Gulf
War. 'What must it have been
like?' maybe in adult brains still. One
wouldn't rate Bush Junior high in Elvis
terms. Perhaps John Lennon
was right when he said Elvis died
early when he joined the Army, but
a divine etiquette does make
any Elvis Elvis, any anxious woman

dancing beside him some protected
firework of unexpected grace.

II. MISSING ELVIS: TWO

All-Ways Winds: Christmas, 2001

Small all-ways winds
in the treetops
bad sign   bad sing   again
                 the fires
two dark red caterpillars
in a small shrugging motion
crawl slowly to each
other on the mountain, there
the night too black for smoke,
                here
at the street's end, the smoke
too black for night.   Small
sudden all-ways winds in trees chant
in waves like a fire, an ocean.
On his way to deep water
'Elvis' the sky-crane helicopter,
looking like a monster
from *Aliens*, flies over
drops spit-spots on the verandah,
hovers to talk, as I look up,
shield my eyes from the molten sunset.

'I've been wanting to ask you', I say,
'whether John Lennon *was* right
and you'd already died
when you entered the army?' The
skycrane says, 'I died in gold pyjamas
up against my bathroom door.
The night before, I was singing
"Through the ages I'll remember
blue eyes crying in the rain."' I ask,
'Will rain come now?' and Elvis
grins, 'Yeah, and it's always more
than you think it'll be, you know, the rain.'
I nod: yes, I know about the rain.
I say, 'I wrote a poem this year, that
any Elvis is Elvis, but didn't expect
this, although I should have. Anyway, what
have you remembered through the ages, why
did you seem to change so much, to lose
humour after they conscripted you? Was
it the Colonel, or something else, some fear
or satire within you?' Elvis thinks, hums
'Blue eyes…love is like a dying ember…'
then considers: 'You know, some
of it was just the diction thing. I got
sick of people asking what I'd sung. The dope
they give you in the army makes you want
to be clear, too…'   'But not like Li'l Abner!'
Elvis asks, 'But didn't the Twin Towers

feel at first like Li'l Abner, or George W.,
in your mind and, baby, don't
we all have some damn mountain—
heart-warm drug and drug of horror—makes
us simple as a soldier for a time? So,
okay, I died in mine.'   To my right,
at Luddenham, Warragamba
the fire's own cumulus clouds
are red at their heart again.

                              Again, the king
considers, 'And, anyway, I consented
to earn millions, be *all* wanted,
just like now.'   The Caravaggio
fat boy all light and shadow
gulping grapes as he once was, slims
        to a skeleton in steel
in the all-ways winds. He cries, 'But
to save the wild life, you gotta
live it—love you, honey!', flies
off like a million U.S. dollars, can
remember something through the ages, if
just the fire's clarity and then
a free confusion of blue mountains, rain.

Southerly

JOHN MATEER

TO NELSON MANDELA

Nelson Rolihlahla Mandela!
Dalibhunga!
Creator-of-Negotiations!
Child-of-Blood!
Thembu Prince!

I am not Thembile Mhlangeni at the opening of Cape Town
      Parliament!
I am not Zolani Mkiva praising at your Inauguration!
My line is not iimbongi!
My line is Jewish-&-English-&-Polish-&-Irish-&-Tristan-de-
      Cunhan-&-Scotch-Unknown!
and now an Aussie voice!
Like Hintsa's head on the huge island the void of Yagan's!
Your praises I can sing as my memory only!

Mandela! in my childhood your name appeared graffitied on a
      suburban wall
Mandela! your Voice was Silence and your Face incredible
      Space
Mandela! you could not be quoted and how many photos of
      you were destroyed
Mandela! you led a march that my father could remember

Mandela! he said you must be a great leader and was
     frightened of you
Mandela! when I first saw you tears poured from me like words
Mandela! I was afraid of offending you with my poem A New
     South Africa
Mandela! Frank-the-Ghanian told me you would probably like
     that criticism
Mandela! Coetzee-the-Critic said he really loves you

Who is the poet and can speak the truth here?
Who can speak and not offend the people in their jubilation?

     The poet as I must address the needed!
     The poet as I must shout out for all creatures!

Mandela! you were like Jesus on the cover of Time magazine
Mandela! at the Sydney Opera House two girls touched your
     hand and said it was like God's
Mandela! on Donahue you were a dignified Being
Mandela! in those secret meetings with PW what did you say?
Mandela! what did you do when you took the helicopter to Big
     Business?
Mandela! and what about the crimson Merc the car the
     workers gave you?
Mandela! and of all those famous and unfamous who've
     grabbed at your robes?

Am I speaking? am I writing here? the pen is not in vain—

You stoop to speak to the small boy calling him 'a big man'
Mandela! when the soccer World Cup was won they reported
Mandela! you danced on your old legs like a young man
     meeting his bride
Mandela! what will Mhlabuhlangene do without you?
Mandela! will the hyaena eat the vulture?

When your bones have gone to meet the Ancestors
and the Europeans' descendants have forgotten who you were
and you are only present in children's names
then I will have prayed your wisdom flowed on like a river of
    genes

    I sing this in good faith,

Nelson Rolihlahla Mandela!
Dalibhunga!
Creator-of-Future!
Careful-Child-of-Humanity's-Cradle!

I disappear!

Overland

LES MURRAY

MELBOURNE PAVEMENT COFFEE

Storeys over storeys without narrative
an estuarine vertical imperative
plugged into vast salt-pans of pavement
and higher hire over the river
ignited words pouring down live:

there an errant dog is running
nose down like a pursuit car
police car! police car! central city
and trams that look always oncoming
stop, and stand simmering like cymbals
after the mesh! of their pair.

Here posture is better, suitings thicker
and footmen are said to survive
behind oaks up the odd gravel drive.
We saw a wall of tomato
blazer-backs striped blue-and-yellow
ranged right across their school stage
just like an inland rain painting.

We heard our grandest parliament sigh
down Bourke Street *My country, why
did you leave me and change at Albury?*
History made here touched the world.
Now a demoted capital bleeds politics
Burnet's immune system was right wing!
down the microphone, black icecream cone,
down the cinecamera, New Age monocle.

Not housing, but characterful houses
lace-trimmed like picnic day blouses
reigned when beer went with cray.
Now the crayfish are Formula One
cars, flat out in raging procession—
but we're off to where the river
learns and teaches the Bay.

Quadrant

JAN OWEN

THE PANGOLINS

(for Mulaika)

Throwing the I Ching by the northern wall
(Mountain over Water: the cataract clears),
rereading the dubious message in dubious light,
dusk there is as brief as thirty years.
The dogs were off at the end of the garden, barking
at moonlight or monkeys, tenor and alto and bass.
Under the rambutans it was lighting-up time—
the teetering lanterns in the leaves and grass

were practising emerald—*becoming, yes, here*;
the fireflies above were loopy with desire.
A pounding of fists south-east from the Surau
was the kampong boys on their Thursday drums. The air
yearned after the odd missed beat like a tired heart.
And then the stranger came. Out of the neat
fit of the dark. Self stood back. No-name
trundled up, snuffling the mulch with her tender snout.

She was the presence of many grandmothers, a homebody
buttressing wonder, nosing around the boles
of the clumped bananas; tip to tapering tip,

a relaxed Bell curve validated with scales
perfectly graded—3:5:8:13…
Her back was firm terrain under my hand,
an equable riddle with a waddle (Earth
over Earth: a friend will be lost, a friend will be found).

I squatted down. She paused and quirked her head:
this was no tree. *To run or not to run?*
To amble. With dignified haste like the shopping-bag rush
for the 5pm to Rawang in Ramadan.
What goes on four legs at night and none at noon?
At dawn alert next day Suwanti chained
the dogs away from a round jungle-green enigma
then bowled the baby into the hedge to its kind.

Quadrant

LOUISE OXLEY

VOICE OVER

After so many days trampling a sea
heavy as his home soil,
reduced to a single intention
like a bottled message
and able to recognise
ten distinct patterns in leeward foam,
he began to draw comfort from the swell
turning to him like the shoulder
of his sleeping wife. Rescued,
he lay on a narrow bunk
treading water, his fractious limbs
still scrawling the urgent translation
of need into action. Submariners
planted their cable-hard hands
on his pillow, leaned over him
with a tenderness they thought
they had forfeited to war, whispered
all was well. Hollowed by the cries
of those left reaching for hand-holds
as they dived for cover, they took turns
to smooth his legs with oil,
drew the blanket up
and crooned old songs.

It was the doctor's silvery
potion of reason that broke his stride.
He was walking now, uphill, along
the line of argument
and it was growing dark.
Someone had ploughed the home paddock
in his absence; breakers of loam
clung to his boots. Upstairs a light was on.
She would be bent to her sewing.
He raised his eyes.

Southerly

GEOFF PAGE

FIVE POEMS FROM 'A GOOD WHEAT PADDOCK SPOILED'

First Edition, The Canberra Times, 3.9.26

I. THE WEATHER WAS ...

The weather was
more metaphoric
in 1926,

extensive rains embracing
the whole of New South Wales
are eagerly predicted.

Who can resist
the slow embrace of rain? Brought, it seems,
by an *energetic disturbance*

approaching from Western Australia.
How do that in metaphor?
A corps of AIF Light Horsemen

transcend the Nullarbor?

II. FIRST FLIGHT

And under PERSONAL, a par
on Stanley Melbourne Bruce, PM,
he of the pinstripe, spats and collar,

making the first
prime minister's hop
from one state to another:

Essendon aerodrome 8:40,
Adelaide at 3.
Some personal friends to see him off

and *representative citizens.*
One sees the wood chocks pulled away,
the biplane taxiing on grass

out into the middle distance.
The great man waves—and they're away.
The ship of state

has taken to the air.

III. A SMELL OF DECENCY

Page 2 is *Sport and Sportsmen*
boxing, soccer, turf and polo
cricket, rugby, Aussie rules,

scratchings from the Caulfield Cup.
The match was very interesting,
it says, between Duntroon and Hall.

Saturdays are all good sense,
a smell of decency, team spirit,
plates of mud thrown up by ponies

galloping in rushes,
the geometries of leather balls
hit or kicked

or run with under arm,
their insides wrought from cork or air.
Naivete or innocence,

it's too late now to tell.
As in the ads down either side:
the gunsmith down in Sydney,

lately of the A.I.F., who says
our hands make good arms
the butcher who in Manuka

knows *how to make both ends meat.*

IV. NEWLANDS SPRINGS

Mattresses and metal beds,
the joys of *Newlands Springs…*
And *Morning Glory* bedding lifts
the soul to higher things.

The *wooden frame* is gone for good.
It never was enough.
The *Newlands* range has guaranteed
No Sagging, Noise or Fluff.

Noiselessness is promised to
all those who hate thin walls.
The *sturdiness of steel* prevents
unseemly midnight falls.

The best hotels around the land
have called in *Newlands Springs*
and mattresses with two aboard
nightly spread their wings.

V. HARRY CRAWFORD, A.I.F.

And Harry Crawford, A.I.F.,
returned,
is found *at two o'clock on Monday afternoon*

inside his workman's tent
on the road out to Weetangera
lying in his bunk with his throat cut.

No suspicious circumstances,
Canberra police say later.
Just that sawing at the throat,

its muscles still resisting,
the right hand going on alone
as if in no-man's-land.

Eight years, it's been, since he came home
swaying down the plank.
Eight years in the 'land for heroes'.

Pozieres comes through at last.

Quadrant

VIVIENNE PLUMB

DRY RISER INLET

You drive just like an er-uncle of mine,
parking well in a tight spot.
Early in the morning I practise my yoga
Sukhasana is easy, *Bakasana* is not.

After lunch you embraced me a little longer
than the others, and last month
you sent me a note that was too familiar.
My favourite pose is *Savasana*,
the corpse position.

The Chicken Palace has become
Super Stock Clearance of Sweets,
I buy a bag of snifters
and force myself to think about you.
The sickly honeysuckle hangs
over the fence in claustrophobic festoons.
Each day I pass Dry Riser Inlet,
the metal fixture on my way to work.

I dream we are making labels
together, that we will stick
on everyone's door.

We live like cosy neighbours
in a New York sit-com style
apartment block. *That will never
happen*, I think in capital letters
when I wake up.

You ring, you send me tiny silk
flowers in hard hot colours, funny
ha ha cards and a packet
of your favourite muesli bars.
Each day I have to pass Dry Riser
Inlet, the safe metal fixture
on my way to work.

Over winter I leave the phone
off its hook, lock the door
and shut the windows.
My arthritis makes it difficult
to do *Halasana* (legs over the head).

Someone says, *your friend left
town.* There is a rumour
that you are teaching English
in Hiroshima. Standing at the stainless

steel sinkbench, I roll the rice
in a banana leaf
and secure it with a sharp
toothpick. Tomorrow
I will change my route to work.

Westerly

PETER PORTER

KOMIKAZE

Each of us thinks he is a suicide
(and we do too, the women say), and this
despite our dread of disappearing
and losing the discipline of self-distaste.

Great then to follow Fundamentalism,
live on forever in the fires of Hell
with all of Evolution pointing to
a point of view which views the point of you.

And Comedy will make it even better—
Saint-Simon's bowels exploding at the Court
and showering shit on ermined sorrowers,
with Heaven laughing at true reverence.

You need to judge the moment to go mad.
Nietzsche heard a tortured horse's scream
and recognised his cue. But Turin now
is just the average sound-frame of complaint.

I'm sure my Father lived so long not out
of fear of death, but more because he knew

he hadn't the profile of the Great and Good
yet wasn't needed where the damned are stowed.

The old joke goes that we sophisticates
will be surprised by hideous prods and pains
from hornèd devils just because we think
such torments silly: already we've seen worse.

Is death a joke? Depends on who is laughing.
I have a friend who tossed into a grave
an avant-garde review to give the corpse
some reading matter for eternity.

Australian Book Review

DAVID PRATER

IN A DIM SEA NATION

she who kills polar bear defends
against the sonic paws of sleep

polar blurs the surfs saturated ice
floes aiming precisely with her still

submerged shotgun she fires twice
& fur sinks into dream beneath us

she who kills polar bear assaults
worm hollows out of the wild space

armed with penetrating flare spots
a soldier camouflaged in white snow

grabs my glassy arm from a floes
thick soup & holds it to her helmet

she who kills polar bear protects
prevents ill joys & the steam sports

constructing perfect depth sleds
out of nothing hidden or down there

in the depths beneath us flies & still
a bear or a dream shark for her boat

she who kills polar bear vanishes
dive bombs ice floes strafing runs

radio contact & then the navys guns
thank god for denmark & the innuit

up shoots the frozen bear buoyantly
a lifesized hole for an arctic ache …

---

papertiger: new world poetry

PETER ROSE

LATE EDITION

Most things are never meant – PHILIP LARKIN, 'Going, Going'

Midnight. A collision threatens
to happen. Sally of breaks.
It procrastinates like an aria,
teasing night editors with their cigarettes.
May never culminate. Interest wanes.
Ignoring the unskilled night
I resume the book of memoirs.
Name-dropping is his genius.
We know each footnote in our
anonymous eyries.
                Again, midnight.
Pedestrians, ubiquitous in scarves,
hasten to the equivocal accident,
never sure what they will disclose.
The cathedral stands idle,
bells strung up like colanders.
Silence. Never such silence.
In another part of the house
you sleep on, oblivious—
dreams that may or may not happen.

Meanjin

DIPTI SARAVANAMUTTU

DINGO TRAILS

An existential vocation after all, being a clown.
Sitting about in windswept places, bits of red dust
and grit making your eyes hurt;
all this shifting chronology, life, worlds,
past the howl of a wild dog and its need to find
a bit of homely earth and lie on it. To breathe.
Occasionally depleted, even brutal,
staring at the garden with an ashy heart.

Write of love and you'll find it, of peace
and it is there. Perhaps we do exist as paradox,
all accidental meanings considered;
asking why, saying it's just your destiny
to stop Charlie Chaplin being chased
permanently out of the room. Not realising
there was even a competition, there's the pity!

It's something like the way what we see
might become us, gentle breadcrumbs scattered
across the front footpath, blue and red rosellas

that sometimes look like accidental gemstones
set within the skeletal parabola of a winter
pear tree, against a darkening silver sky.

The Age

MICHAEL SHARKEY

THE ADVANTAGES OF DAUGHTERS

Daughters are convenient for fathers who perceive that other
      fathers
Have an interest in their daughters.

Now they do not have to wonder how it felt to other parents of
      neat daughters,
Not so far back, even recently sometimes, when they snuck
      glances

At those other parents' children. Checking out how noses, ears
      and mouths
And eyes and lengths of feet and hair etcetera came to fit.

Daughters are unparalleled for triggering thoughts like that.
They are also good for meditation on the paradox of grace,

And in their charity they help their parents comprehend
Postmodern sex, when parents come home early and discover
      daughters

Deep in exploration of their sexual orientation with the local
      pastor's help,
Undressed and tantric on the lounge room floor. Don't ask.

Daughters are superlative for running down their parents
Until someone does it better. Then they turn to savage beasts.

Or they agree. Daughters have amazing untapped talents for
    intuiting
That someone they've been talking to long distance for three
    hours

Is a bore. Daughters are adept at making time seem like
    eternity
When bathrooms are required and they're in them.

When the will obliterates experience, they offer 'No one here
    cares
What I think.' 'Boring' is the first word daughters learn,

And then they travel, till the word becomes concrete. They
    have gifts
That people with vast projects find amazing, like a genius for

Overcoming weariness: they hone this through long practice,
    snapping-to
At 1 a.m., when someone phones to say the party's on what's
    keeping you.

Daughters know the end of evolution is a male
That puts himself out with the garbage.

Daughters are exquisite at expanding parents' consciousness
Of ways that money circulates in hotels, clubs and bars.

They're also good for leaving subtle clues like shoes and
        documents,
Devices made in Denmark, and addresses in strange bedrooms,

So that other persons' parents are the first to know
That families of such daughters are about to be genetically
        enhanced

Or have their physical condition modified. Daughters are
        invaluable
For colonising rooms, when they call back to stay an evening,

So that objects in the middens they create can reappear in
        later years
To feed nostalgia when the comedy of cleaning up has passed.

Daughters are magnificent, on visiting from living years abroad,
For mothers who admire to be told that times have changed, in
        case

Nobody here has noticed. Daughters are surpassing for
        reminding anyone
Who likes to know that Elle MacPherson is not what all women
        look like.

And her brand of clothes suits only older women. Daughters
    have an extra
Seven years of life expectancy, compared with sons and fathers
    who instead

Have the excitement of knowing that they're bound for
    obsolescence.
Daughters feel compelled to act as memory, since no parent
    can recall

Such simple facts. Daughters are unmatched for bringing good
    news
To the home. 'Last night he moved out and now he's living
    with his secretary.

He always was a creep.' No matter that they've been advised
    since birth
To live with women, and give men the flick. At other times,

They bring in odd-shaped children, saying 'This is your new
    grandchild,
Will you mind it?' then rush out with 'There's this new man
    that I've met,

I think it's serious.' At times they bring weird adults, whom
    they introduce
As D.J. who is working at the gym, or 'This is Butch who trains
    Rottweilers.'

He does tattoos on the side. Their men are hopeless, always
        waiting
For the right job, as if anyone needs jobs, they say and grin at
        you,

While making notes of just how far they pushed you,
Till your eyes said go and die a long slow death, but
        somewhere else.

It isn't that they love to torment women (and they do), but
        that one day,
When writs are flying (and they will be), that sweet child the
        monster's with now

Might imagine you approved. For the moment, in the
        playground,
Where the child is eating ice-cream and reflecting on the
        compliments

The people in the Indian ice-cream shop provide with
        ice-cream (seven flavours:
Mango, cardamom, pistachio … banana best of all she says,
        definitive),

The clouds come hauling shadows through the park, where
        pigeons glide
Among the nikau and a possum snores contentedly in daylight,

And the wind is in unequalled form, as fathers look abstracted,
Now and then observing how the arms and eyes etcetera make
a daughter.

Famous Reporter

R. A. SIMPSON

JOURNEYS UNDER THE CITY

In the underground of nerves
every station is very brief

but a breakdown in chilly darkness
may last a year or more
before the wheels can grind again

and ever so slowly you are freed
into the rounded open mouth
full of daylight

The worst journey doesn't end
the train stays terribly still a lifetime
makes wide-eyed passengers
pace up and down the corridors
trying to force immovable doors
then squash their faces against the windows
one distorted like a child mocking

you'll stay like that

The Age

ALEX SKOVRON

ONCE WE CROSSED THE EQUATOR

Once we crossed the Equator
we understood that we could never turn back
for all the seabirds were flowing in the opposite direction
and the disturbance we created
in the air and on the water was always behind us
the sea an endless terrain of low peaks and ranges
flowing, falling, rising until snow broke out on their crests
the breeze awash with a strange exhausted vibrancy
the motors' throbbing below us a dull obbligato
the portholes clear and free of reflections
for the sun too was behind us
and if not behind us then asleep somewhere
behind the clouds with their fantastical topography
through which glimmers of naïve colour remotely whispered

When we crossed into the Tropics
the light changed, and suddenly the vessel's surfaces
its polished timbers and quaint panelling
took on a novel sheen, peculiar images appeared
at first faint effigies of memories we had not yet dreamed
then gradually colours and curves that intoxicated
the more we attached our hungry gaze to their geography

and we knew we would need to possess them
and we knew we never could
because the seabirds and the clouds
and the engines' low insistence told us so

As we crossed into the Polar regions
we discovered we could no longer discern the birds
the water became mere ripples
like the breath of a sleeping infant
the air had lifted and the clouds assumed a snowy radiance
it was colder here of course
but there were rumours that the sun was expected
that the mechanical hum would be stilled
that the brittle ice flowing, falling, rising around us
until the pieces joined and fused into each other
would slowly melt and sink
amid all the other prophecies of our past

and we could proceed in silence
unencumbered by dreams and imaginings
our horizon shining and almost touchable beyond
our vessel's lengthening shadow
towards the Equator

Salt

PETER SKRZYNECKI

THE THIRD FACE IN THE PHOTOGRAPH

Posed by the photographer
from *The Sydney Morning Herald*
for an article to appear
in 'Summer Agenda',
I stand behind my seated mother
 in the front garden
of the house
that was my home
until I moved away in 1967.

'No, it's not right',
says the photographer, a Cork man.
'You need to be holding
something…A book, yes.
Have you got
a book with you?'

I go and bring
the only book I have in my car—
the *Selected Poems 1965–75*
of an Irish poet.

Without knowing it,
I hold the book, front cover out.

My mother sits in clothes
she's made herself.
She has combed her hair.
Her hands are folded,
palms up, as if meditating.
You can see the bent fingers.
The veins are like roots
reaching into soil.
Although she's smiling,
her seventy-nine-year-old face
looks absent, withdrawn.
It's like she isn't there.

It will be the last photograph
taken of my mother
and myself—on the lawn
that my father weeded
so diligently and mowed.
The redbrick veneer façade of
10 Mary Street, Regents Park,
will be captured
in a city's newspaper—
'an opportunity' my father

would have shrugged off, dismissed
as being unimportant.

The last photograph
of a mother and son—
with a third face staring
back at the camera
from the cover of a book:

the stranger, hair windblown,
wearing a parka,
jaw set, barely smiling—
indomitable, chiselled,
almost Stone Age—
squinting into the light,
his back to a shoreline
at low tide—

himself, like mother and son,
caught forever
with two strangers
on the film of a camera
that never misses its subject
once the focus is set.

Quadrant

NORMAN TALBOT

THE RESURRECTION AT COOKHAM

(from 'The Resurrection' by Stanley Spencer)

Stan was used to the quiet church at Cookham,
the mute graveyard that the Parson calls 'cemetery'.
He painted faithfully weddings, christenings, burials,
but he couldn't get used to the Bible!

Stan was accustomed to death, to sold separations,
from his earliest years. That all-gone factual loss,
that covering of leftovers with lid, soil & sod…
But how can he get used to this other, impossible story?

Let's see then, said Stan, nodding to recent neighbours,
who's been bricked up here, under all this ivy,
this living holdfast? Let that old geezer there
out of his railings: he'll be one of Em's family.

That drowsy lady with two babes-in-arms,
a Big House servant—or from the Parsonage.
Who'll come out of the little grave there? Who's who behind
the narrow illegible stone? Who's where two rosebushes run wild?

All the way down to the river, little boneyard mounds
crack open like unstamped eggs. But back up here
that mannered Palladian stone tomb was for an 'Old Family'
(the last Big House but one: Stan knows them only from Adam).

God knows who's rising from that black sunk oldest patch,
the first bit of ground they blessed...Housethanes &
     strongthieves—
or maybe saints—brave bones all, some of them very bare!
Their one last stand. Any odder than flesh coming back?

Let's tip the coffins on end as they rear out of the earth,
that'll help. Some bodies stretch & yawn, some help the others,
the ones that stagger widdershins. In the hallelujah light
you blink to believe, and the painter of flesh blinks most.

How could this be? How could the horror-feel be fled
from death & corruption? Can rot be ploughed back
into the permasoil? Keep it simple: will Parson still wear
his lawn sleeves or not? It did Stan good to play that.

Heat

JOHN TRANTER

BRUSSELS

After Rimbaud

The eagle who kills with lightning
idles in a palace smothered by flowers.
Of course he is never seen. The sky above is
pale green and Saharan blue, shreds and patches of it
peeping between the dark leaves…

it must be the Cote d'Azur, it must be fast cars,
idle young men inflamed by gasoline!
And when the exhaust note had faded, why,
calm returns, the last century returns, my
abandoned world returns, the world I have lost,

the life I threw away, the Juliet I neglected—
can any of that be recovered? Blue devils
topple from gliders into a pattern: parachutes,
idols, descending…history is this delicious day
over and done—old orchards: forgotten fruit.

Now the waterfront, patrolled by helicopters,
where monkeys dance, guitars pluck at the air,
children in red makeup clutch at your sleeve,

and, looking down from a secluded window
a beautiful woman dazed by magazines...

paying for an exclusive suite done out
like a library, books bound in buckram, so she can
doze on a divan, nothing more useful: nothing
more ravishing that her vulnerable sleep—let us
creep and whisper! Below, a cul-de-sac choked with

expensive shops towards whose glow and glitter
her soul inclines, whose chandeliers illuminate
her heaven, whose throngs act out a million dramas
curt, cruel, and concentrated, just for her: I dwell on it—
be jealous!—and adore it in silence.

The Age

Xuan Duong

THE JULY RAIN

The rain cheerfully visits the grapefruit tree
the grapefruit is away
collecting flowers from a far off land

the rain then goes to the beehive
the bees are lying drunk from honey
the rain shakes the peppercorn
the peppercorn busy washing hair

the rain showers the maple tree
the maple is in a coma
the rain drops on the coral tree
the coral is nursing its sore bones

the rain rests on the betel leaves
the betel leaves are missing the ants
the rain waltzes to the ferry
the ferry is being deserted
being frustrated, friendless and lonely

marches to the Boat People Sea
the rain activates the ocean

the rain mobilizes the sky
into looking for lost boats of refugees

follows then
a broken piece of timber
drifting in the remote water.

Overland

MARIA ZAJKOWSKI

THE GREY MARE THE BETTER HORSE

Sunday, 5.30, there through the Cosmos
she attends to Silver Beet, unslung as an ironing board
stuck in the peat while the old cat watches,
his black cheeks round as a weird sun.

Higher up in the brain of the day, air is cooler
and real birds in seasonal arrows head for a tune.
Her Turkish neighbour delivers fatty smoke through the trees—
the whole world's a barbecue (some little dog disagrees).

Camouflaged in cloud shadow she uncurls up,
fountains of garlic applaud, her black curls nod back
and at the house; its flaky ancience and odd pipes good
for another life, maybe two, whatever stands it.

The whole family's out next door, barking up the day,
calling ages out, calling, yelling, laughing into the absorbent
        evening.
From his post the old Tom sees night in
as she deals out her dinner under the electric light,

with its bulb she converses and later dances in the swinging
    breeze.
Cotton clean she irons herself, checks her face in a pan
and, taking drinks into the garden, to night-flowers proposes
a toast to 'us'.

Heat

CONTRIBUTORS' NOTES

ROBERT ADAMSON has successfully combined the careers of writer, editor and publisher. From 1970 to 1985 he edited *New Poetry* magazine, and in 1988, with Juno Gemes, he established Paper Bark Press. He has been the recipient of many awards and prizes, including the National Book Council's Banjo Award, The New South Wales Literary Award's Kenneth Slessor Prize, and the Victorian Premier's Literary Award for poetry. In 1994 he was awarded the F.A.W. Christopher Brennan prize for lifetime achievement in literature.

Of 'Elegy', Adamson writes: 'Death is something I can't understand and yet most of my poems these days are elegies. Elegies and love poems: they are connected, singing to people who can no longer hear you, trying to look back to where you think the person the elegy's about is. Time and tide wait for no one; I can't understand exactly what time is but the tides ebb and flow for sure. Words are almost as mysterious as time. We can hear the music without words but we certainly can't hear the songs. Instead of living in denial of death we must learn to embrace it, try to imagine a song that could make a stone hear'.

JORDIE ALBISTON was born in Melbourne in 1961. Her first poetry collection *Nervous Arcs* (Spinifex, 1995) won first prize in the Mary Gilmore Award, second in the Anne Elder Award, and was shortlisted for the NSW Premier's Award. Her second book was entitled *Botany Bay Document: A Poetic History of the Women of Botany Bay* (Black Pepper, 1996). Her most recent collection, *The Hanging of Jean Lee* (Black Pepper, 1998), explores the life and death of the last woman hanged in Australia (1951). Jordie received the Dinny O'Hearn Memorial Fellowship in 1997 and was the original editor of the first all-Australian all-poetry e-zine, *Divan*. She holds a Ph.D in literature, and her fourth poetry book *The Fall* will be released in 2003.

Of 'Apostrophe', Albiston writes: 'One meaning of the word "apostrophe" is "a figure of speech in which a thing, a place, an idea, a dead or absent person, is addressed as if present and capable of understanding". I wrote this poem to myself, the dead inner self, which no longer seemed capable of writing or creating. I wanted to move in concentric circles from the wider view of "us" (first stanza), through the objective view of "you" (second stanza), and into the subjective view of "self" (final stanza). The poem is an angry one, and I have written into it some of the bitterness, cynicism and disappointment I held towards myself, and towards poetry—as an answer—at the time. Of course, thinking about it now, I can see the irony in putting such feelings straight into another poem…'.

JOHN ALLISON was born in New Zealand in 1950 and now lives in the Dandenong Ranges east of Melbourne. His poems have been published in many journals worldwide. He was the featured poet in *Poetry New Zealand 14*, and has had three books of poetry published: *Dividing the Light* (Hazard Press, 1997); *Both Roads Taken* (Sudden Valley Press, 1997); and *Stone Moon Dark Water* (Sudden Valley Press, 1999). His book *A Way of Seeing: perception, imagination and poetry* will be published by Lindisfarne Press in the USA in May 2003.

Of 'Towards the Horizon', Allison writes: 'I often come across these aphoristic phrases in my reading—on this occasion, a Swedish poet, Emerson, and Leonardo da Vinci. I usually enter them in my journal, and at some point, in relation to some experience, it's as if they start talking to each other. The juxtapositions of this dialogue open up an imaginative space, a "heightening", when the world and self seem to become something other in a momentary epiphany. When this poem was completed I thought, "That's it!" The adrenalin rush when I stepped back from the writing desk and had to go out for a walk, excited in the world and the word—fascinated by the power of transformation, that sudden shift of consciousness disrupting the usual, like lightning clearing the air—this was my test of the poem'.

JUDITH BEVERIDGE was born in England in 1956 and came to Australia in 1960. She has published two books of poetry, *The Domesticity of Giraffes* (Black Lightning Press, 1987) and *Accidental Grace* (University of Queensland Press, 1996), and has also co-edited an anthology of Australian poetry, *A Parachute of Blue* (Round Table Publications, 1996). Her work has been also been translated into several languages and has been set for HSC study. A new volume *Wolf Notes* will appear in 2003.

Of 'Whisky Grass', Beveridge writes: 'Whisky Grass *(Andropogon virginicus)* is a common weed grass around the Sydney area. I've always loved the combination of these two words. The poem grew from the first line after a bout of anxiety had laid me low for awhile. I was looking for a way to describe the experience without becoming too self-referential, and I ended up drawing on images gleaned from my experience as a Bush Regenerator and thus was able to play off both a sense of degradation and reparation. The challenge with this poem was to use a dense form, yet also to maintain a flexible and resonant rhythm and avoid becoming melodramatic. One of the ways I tried to achieve this was to break the lines at perhaps unexpected points and to let the tension do its job'.

KEN BOLTON was born in Sydney (1949) and lives in Adelaide, where he is associated with the Experimental Art Foundation. He is a poet, art critic, and also an editor and publisher, currently producing the Little Esther books series. He edited the magazines *Otis Rush* and *Magic Sam*. His major publications include *Selected Poems* (Penguin/ETT) and *Untimely Meditations* (Wakefield Press). A recent title is *August 6th* (Little Esther). His art criticism has been widely published. He has written (and published) a great deal of collaborative poetry with Melbourne poet John Jenkins, including

The Wallah Group (Little Esther) and *Nutters Without Fetters* (Press Press). Ken Bolton edited *Homage To John Forbes*, published by Brandl & Schlesinger in 2002.

Of 'A Prospect of the Young KB as a Critic', Bolton writes: 'The first thing to say about the poem is that it's a sestina: a form that enforces a certain number of repetitions: the end words of the first six lines must reappear throughout in strictly prescribed order. They are a bit of a head-twist to do—which is where the difficulty and the fun come in. I hope usually for a nutty result, though it's probably a good form for mourning in or for neurosis. Maybe this poem has some of both. Otherwise it's pretty straightforward. It describes the memory of a Sunday morning reading the comix pages and wishing for a more exciting life, a more sophisticated life, too, evidently. I was too young for either. I can never remember what the poem is called—"Sunday, Bloody Sunday" or "Sunday Bloody Critic" is how I remember it. Its real title links it to similarly titled poems by Ashbery and Marvell'.

PETER BOYLE was born in Melbourne in 1951. He has lived most of his life in Sydney where he works as a teacher with TAFE. He has written three collections of poems, *Coming home from the world* (Five Islands Press, 1994), *The Blue Cloud of Crying* (Hale and Iremonger, 1997), and *What the painter saw in our faces* (Five Islands Press, 2001). He has also translated poetry from Spanish and French. A collection of his translations from Venezuelan poet Eugenio Montejo is forthcoming from Salt Publishing.

Of 'Nearness', Boyle writes: 'In the ongoing effort to stave off depression, bleakness and collapse, a poem may be less a report on anything than a battleground between life's ever-gathering gloom and the instinct for hope, beauty. So, I think, with this poem. The small woman with dark hair who spins at the centre of the whirlwind may be forever unobtained and unobtainable but, at least within the poem, her face and the mysterious book she offers suggest that I don't have to go under yet. In a prison a poem may be a place of freedom, rejecting Auden's saying that "nothing is beautiful, not even in poetry, that is not the case." I wrote this poem in the winter of 2001, not really understanding what it might mean but totally enjoying its strangeness'.

GARY CATALANO was born in Brisbane in 1947. He is the author of eight books of poetry, including *The Empire of Grass* for which he won the Grace Leven Prize in 1992. He was the art critic for *The Age* between 1985 and 1990 and, in 1997, he held a residency at the Australia Council's Keesing Studio in Paris. He wrote several major books on Australian art and art criticism, including *The Solitary Watcher: Rick Amor and his Art* (2001). He died in 2002 after a long illness.

JENNIFER COMPTON was born in New Zealand in 1949. She now lives in Wingello, on the Southern Highlands of NSW, with her husband and children. Her stage play *The Big Picture* premiered at the Griffin Theatre in Sydney, and is published by Currency Press. And her book of poetry, *Blue*, published by Ginninderra Press, was shortlisted for the NSW Premier's Award in 2001.

Of 'Castle', Compton writes: 'I had a vivid dream about someone who lived a long time ago. I was particularly interested, during my dream, and afterwards, when I woke, that the mind and body that had inhabited me during this time was male. And in the perspective this person had on his place in society. After some time of being peripherally aware of him, like the friend who has gone overseas and doesn't keep in touch, it occurred to me that maybe I could write a poem for him. Or write his poem. The one he couldn't write. The first line came about because I asked him what his name was. The first time I read this poem in public I felt inhabited by him again, and almost choked as I looked up from the page and saw the people sitting in front of me. The line—'As I walked across the meadow towards you'—took on a strange curve. Because these were the people he had been walking towards for such a long time'.

MTC CRONIN has had nine books of poetry published, the most recent being *beautiful, unfinished ~ PARABLE/SONG/CANTO/*

POEM (Salt Publishing, Cambridge, UK, 2003). She lives with her partner, a musician, and their three young daughters.

Of 'The Flower, The Thing', Cronin writes: 'Sitting on the steps of a house in Enmore—surrounded by city, a part of the city—the poet, Greg McLaren, and I discussed the desire to write, the impossibility of writing, *a* thing without writing *about* the thing. (And here I am writing a thing about the thing for another thing!) In my folders of "scraps" I have a photocopied page, *Aa* to *Gg*, accompanied by hieroglyphics perhaps. I don't know where the page is from and what it is really about though it seems to show the development of sounds, language, writing…It's a mystery to me though I've written many poems whilst sitting looking at it. On it is a rope, a tether, a vulture, a jar…Things which might be archetypes, which resonate…Flowers also are a mystery to me. This poem is one in my *Book of Flowers & Dedications*. Currently there are over 230 of them, all (except one) 25 lines long, all dedicated to someone living or dead, real or fictional. Why write about flowers when I know little about them? To partake of the mystery that is poetry. Also, they are my poetic meditation, a pleasure that is unaware of its content. Kate Fagan, another poet (*Dustflower!*), refers to them as my *21st Century Florilegium*. And did you know that "anthology" and 'posy' are two words which have somehow, over time, swapped their meanings?'

STEPHEN EDGAR was born in Sydney in 1951 but has lived in Hobart since 1974. He is the author of five collections of poetry, the latest being *Lost in the Foreground* (Duffy & Snellgrove, 2003).

Of 'Eighth Heaven', Edgar writes: 'I have forgotten the origins of many poems but this one I can remember and it is an interesting example of the disparate sources which can give rise to a poem, as well as of the view (Borges's?) that literature is not separate from life but part of it. I had been re-reading Dante and had finished *Paradiso*; I had also been reading a novel by Julia Blackburn called *The Book of Colour*, a dreamlike work about "family history and the peculiar spells of memory". I then reread the novel's epigraph from *Return from Death* by Derick Thompson:

> *When I came back from death*
> *it was morning*
> *the back door was open ...*

Under the influence of these three pieces of writing I began to think about my childhood'.

MICHAEL FARRELL was born in Bombala and lives in Melbourne. He is the Australian editor of *slope* and the author of *ode ode* (Salt Publishing, 2003).

Of 'Sydney', Farrell writes: 'I was reading *Letters From Iceland* and Marianne Moore's *Complete Poems* when I wrote the poem. I was visiting Sydney. The poem was an attempt at an equivalent of Moore's "New York", as well as an attempted portrait of Sydney. The struggle I had with the poem was avoiding what sounded to me as the satirical, and some lines/images were cut to try to neutralise the tone'.

PHILIP HAMMIAL has had 15 collections of poetry published. His fourteenth, *Bread*, from Black Pepper, was shortlisted for the NSW Premier's Prize for Poetry in 2001. He is also a sculptor, having had 22 solo exhibitions since 1986, and is Director of The Australian Collection of Outsider Art.

Hammial writes: '"Everlastingness", like most of my poems, was written in what, for lack of a better term, I'll call a trance. It was *given*, complete with punctuation, etc, in just a few minutes. And having *received* it, I made no alterations. Looking at it after the fact, I can see that it incorporates several incidents from a 66-year-long life. I first went to Florence in '58 and did buy the filigree furniture for my mother. After she passed away it came back to me. And I've been to Tibet, twice, in '84 and '86. The Alexander David-Neel reference is from one of her books that I read at least thirty years ago, and the I.G. Farben/Harz Mountains reference is from a Thomas Pynchon novel, also read many years ago. The "humping stones from a quarry" is a reference to a visit I made to a concentration camp in Austria in '73. And as a student of Tibetan Buddhism since 1958, I've long been fascinated by the Chöd ritual that is associated with a tantric practice for experienced adepts. I suppose many hard-nosed Australian poets would find my method of writing—in trance, as a medium, an oracle—hopelessly romantic and old-fashioned, but I couldn't care less'.

JENNIFER HARRISON is a Melbourne poet and child psychiatrist. Her most recent poetry collection, *Dear B*, was short-listed for the 1999 Age Book of the Year, the 1999 NSW Premier's Award and the inaugural Judith Wright Poetry Prize. She is currently working on her fourth collection assisted by a literary grant from the Australia Council.

Harrison writes: '"Funambulist" is part of a series of poems and photographs thematically concerned with Australian and European street theatre traditions. The funambulist is a ropewalker or ropedancer and the poem was inspired by a comedy duo called Highly Strung, seen at the Port Fairy Folk Festival in 1998. The clowns perceived themselves as part of a new wave of circus entertainers who had left the big tent for outdoor ropewalking—this allowed them greater interaction with audiences, particularly children. Other performers have inspired various images in the poem; for example, the line "faked fight of the fist on the drum" came from observing a drum busker in Swanston Street, Melbourne in 2000. "Funambulist" has, I think, an air of tenuousness, yet of balance maintained. Clowns mutate with the times like cartoons representing all the madness and humour of our lives. I liked the idea of clowns as "beamed upon" gods—no problem too big or small to tackle. Children love that. The form of the poem, and some images, were inspired by Kay Dick's book *Pierrot* in which she lists the things Pierrot carried in medieval times. The poem evolves into a rather surreal list poem. It was written quickly and preserves some of the energy of the ropedancer in the rhythm'.

MIKE HEALD was born in Grimsby, England in 1959. His family moved to Perth, Western Australia, in 1972. He studied English at the University of WA, completing a Ph.D in contemporary poetry in 1998. During his time as a student he also worked, in Australia and Europe, as a professional squash player. He presently teaches Literature at Trinity College, Melbourne University, and lives in Ballarat.

Heald writes: 'The poem "Fire" was written at a time when I was involved with a group trying to prevent logging in our local forest. It had been a hot summer, and arguments were put that logging reduces the risk of bush fires. In fact, the opposite is true, as many inquiries have found. Another important impetus was the idea of fire, which is held by some cultures as having its existence somewhere between the human realm and that of the gods: as being superhuman, as it were, but not divine. That idea seemed to allow me to formulate a "character" for fire that I could address'.

CLIVE JAMES has published verse throughout his career, whether as poetry for the page or as lyrics for the singer and composer Pete Atkin. In 2003 they toured both Britain and Australia with a showcase of their songs. Their albums can be obtained direct from www.peteatkin.com. As a poet, James published his collected poems under the title of *Other Passports* in 1986. A much-expanded version appeared in late 2003 under the title of *The Book of My Enemy*.

James writes: 'I agree with Robert Graves that poems should make their journey, whether to eternity or to oblivion, without the benefit or the burden of explanatory notes. But in 2002, when touring Britain with Pete Atkin, I read out the newly composed "Occupation: Housewife" as part of my share in the act, and I found that for the younger members in the audience it was useful to be told in advance that the Toni was a home permanent wave kit and that Vim was the sort of revolutionary cleansing agent that had to be advertised in the 1940s with pictures of germs being attacked by little soldiers with swords. These were international products but their time had passed. Another reference was specifically Australian: "reffo" as the slang word for "refugee". Luckily the word is no longer current even in the land of its coinage, so I am quite glad that it brooks a preliminary explanation on stage. On the page, however, there are no explanations necessary, I hope. I waited more than forty years to write this poem and if all the relevant information isn't in there along with the emotion then I didn't write it properly'.

JUDY JOHNSON was born on Anzac Day, 1961, and she would heartily recommend being brought into the world on a public holiday because the birthee always gets a day off school/work on her birthday. She has been writing poetry for fifteen years while rearing three children (not one of whom was born on a public holiday, sadly). Her first collection of poetry *Wing Corrections* came second in the Anne Elder Award, was set for the Year 11 literature list in WA, and is on its second print run. Her second collection won the Wesley Michel Wright Prize and is forthcoming from Black Pepper Press. She won the 2002 Josephine Ulriçk Poetry Prize, the Arts Queensland 2002 Val Vallis Award, the 2001 Bruce Dawe Poetry Prize, the Roland Robinson Award and The Tom Collins Poetry Prize, twice. She completed a mentorship with Dorothy Porter several years ago, which led to a verse novel, supported by an Australia Council grant. Currently she is writing an historical prose novel about a female Anglican Missionary in Papua in 1926.

Of 'Self Pity', Johnson writes: 'I've been reading James Frey's *How to Write Damn Good Fiction* because my current preoccupation is a novel (not to be confused with my perennial love, which is poetry!). What he says about compelling prose pertains to what I wanted to accomplish in "Self Pity" (the second of three sections in my long poem "The African Spider Cures"). Of "The Fictive Dream State", Frey holds that the sense of immersion a reader experiences in good writing results from the power of suggestion—he parallels writer with hypnotist and fine writing with a hypnotic trance. I wanted the narrator in "The African

Spider Cures" to be didactic, but also persuasive and ironic. That was why I used long lines: so that the mesmeric qualities of the voice could continue relatively undisturbed by line breaks. I think of the poem as instructions to the reader on how to build a mirror. Once the mirror is built, the glass in place, the framework testable in the real world, then what readers see when they look into it is up to them'.

AILEEN KELLY was born in England, graduated from Cambridge University, and has spent most of her adult life in Melbourne, working as an adult educator. Her first book, *Coming up for Light*, won the Mary Gilmore Award and was shortlisted for the Anne Elder and Victorian Premier's Poetry Awards. The Vincent Buckley Prize, extended by a VicArts grant, enabled her to spend three months writing in Ireland in 1998. Her work is widely published in journals in Australia and elsewhere, and her latest book is *City and Stranger* (Five Islands Press, 2002).

Of 'Whirlpool', Kelly writes: 'One of the strengths of recent Australian poetry seems to me to be the complexity of roots and of voices for those who are migrants or the children of migrants. I see this in my own work in ways that readers may not even notice, but there are some poems, like "The Whirlpool", which deal directly with this area. There is a double sense of rich heritage and of dislocation that, I think, may be closer to the surface for migrants, but is actually about the human condition in general: "divine discontent", "no lasting habitation", feelings of commonality and isolation and difference, and a strong but troubled desire to claim family, culture and place. In this poem it emerged in the most natural way, imaged in the tumbled ancestries and locations and wonderfully disparate bird-life of my own history'.

JOHN KINSELLA's *Selected and New Poems: Peripheral Light* will appear with W.W. Norton and Fremantle Arts Centre Press in late 2003. He is a Fellow at Churchill College, Cambridge University, and Professor of English at Kenyon College, USA.

Of 'Lyrical Unification in Gambier', Kinsella writes: 'A poem that was largely composed in my head as I travelled in a car between Columbus, the capital city of Ohio, and the village of Gambier where I teach at Kenyon College in the United States. The driver was recounting local storm stories, and I was listening to these as well as thinking about Marjorie Perloff's essay on "Language Poetry and the Lyric Subject". In essence, it's a dialogue with this essay, and the lyrical impulse stimulated by travelling through a rural area at once similar to the ones I have written about all my life, and stunningly different. It's a corn place of red barns: no obvious salinity, no fields of wheat, and very few sheep. The poem is a meditation on the fragmentary nature of the lyrical self, and the intertextual but often conflicting strands that want to force themselves into a composition, whether they sit comfortably or not. Textual language becomes the thread that holds impressions and ideas together, but it also generates its own set of meanings. In a sense, it's a poem that represents a crisis in poetics for me: a case of the "centre cannot hold", and the compulsion to look elsewhere for "sense"'.

BRONWYN LEA was born in Tasmania in 1969 and grew up in Queensland and Papua New Guinea. She studied Literature at California State University in San Diego (where she lived for 12 years) and is currently completing a doctorate in writing at the University of Queensland. She is the author of *Flight Animals* (University of Queensland Press, 2001) and lives in Brisbane with her daughter, Tia.

Of 'These Gifts', Lea writes: 'In much the same way that a lot of love poems are, this poem was born of wishful thinking. I wrote it not at summer's end but at its height, that week in January when the Queensland sun gets unbearable. Around this time I was struck by the number of poems entitled 'The Gift' or some slight variation. I started counting and came up with close to a hundred on my bookshelves alone: Hafiz, Frost, Milosz, HD, Olds, Momaday, Hewitt, Gray, Shapcott, McCauley, Douglas Stewart, Malouf among others. I wrote an essay about it. Then I wrote this poem'.

GEOFFREY LEHMANN was born in 1940, graduated from the University of Sydney in Arts and Law, practised as a solicitor when he graduated, and eventually owned a small law firm until 1976, when he went to teach law in the Commerce Faculty at the University of New South Wales. He taught there until the start of 1986, eventually specialising in taxation law, when he joined an accounting firm as a tax technical director, and in 1990 became a partner of Pricewaterhouse, now PricewaterhouseCoopers. On his retirement from the partnership at age 60, he continued as Tax Counsel of PricewaterhouseCoopers, a full-time role which he still holds. He has been married twice, and from his first marriage he has three children, Julia, John and Lucy. From his second marriage, with his wife, Gail Pearson, he has two sons, Nicholas and Harold, who are the subjects of 'Father and Sons'.

About 'Father and Sons', Lehmann writes: 'For most of my life I have written a poem in a single sitting, or if it was a longer poem, over some months, but with a clear idea of where it was headed, and how the poem would look. This method of writing a poem does not preclude frequent revision often years later. The single sitting way of writing a poem has as its aesthetic the idea that a poem is given to the poet in a singular moment of inspiration. That moment may of course be spread over several days, as the inspiration sorts itself out and the poem takes shape. Allied to this idea is a view that poems cannot be invented or fabricated. Poets may often fabricate or fake poems, and part of the process of editing is to eliminate the fakes. 'Father and Sons' is one of a handful of poems I have written using, what is for me, a new way of writing poetry. It started by accident. I wrote short poems, very short poems, about family life over a period of years, without any sense of direction, and not knowing how they would turn out. I realised that each of these short poems, by itself, was not sustainable. As I wrote each one, I hoped that something would come along, some day, which would somehow allow each short poem to be joined to the others and become a meaningful whole. I was attracted by the niggardliness of these short poems, yet each was too spare by itself to be a self-contained whole. Some lyrical more expansive gesture was needed to bring them together. In 'Father and Sons' the break-through was XII. I knew then that after many years of assembling these fragments I had a poem'.

EMMA LEW was born in Melbourne in 1962. She has published two collections of poetry: *The Wild Reply* (Black Pepper, 1997) and *Anything the Landlord Touches* (Giramondo, 2002). She lives in Richmond with her husband and their dog.

Of 'The Clover Seed Hex', Lew writes: 'I'd broken my ankle and had to spend a few weeks lying on the couch all day. The poems poured out, and this was one of them. At the time I was reading a lot about the Middle East. In Egypt, to say that something is like a cube of sugar is to say it is very beautiful'.

JENNIFER MAIDEN was born in Penrith, N.S.W. in 1949. She has had fourteen books published: poetry and two novels. She has won the N.S.W. Premier's Literary Award twice, the Victorian Premier's Literary Award, the Harry Jones Prize, the Henry Lawson Festival Prize, the Southerly English Association Prize and the Christopher Brennan Award for lifetime achievement in literature. Her latest collection, *Mines*, was published by Paper Bark Press in 1999. She is working on a new collection, which includes 'Missing Elvis'.

Maiden writes: 'Without wishing to impinge on individual reader interpretation, some of the elements worth considering in 'Missing Elvis' might be its treatment of public personalities as useful, evocative nouns rather than sacrosanct entities, and its juxtaposition of realities and concepts often not associated (or with an association usually verbal but here made three-dimensional) to question hierarchical and doctrinaire assumptions, put them in a more humane and balanced psychological, artistic and political perspective with consequent or parallel breaking down of categorisation. As well as developed juxtaposition (what I have sometimes called "Cluster Poems"), lyricism, narrative and humour and also meant to achieve these humane, artistic and critical goals'.

JOHN MATEER was born in South Africa. He has published four books of poems in Australia: *Loanwords* (Fremantle Arts Centre Press, 2002), *Barefoot Speech* (winner of the Victorian Premier's Literary Award, Fremantle Arts Centre Press, 2000), *Anachronism* (Fremantle Arts Centre Press, 1997), and *Burning Swans* (Fremantle Arts Centre Press, 1994). He has also published a number of chapbooks in Australia, South Africa and Indonesia, the most recent of which is *Makwerekwere* (The Zero Press, 2002). The collection he wrote while living in Japan in 2002–3, *The Ancient Capital of Images*, is forthcoming in 2003.

Of 'To Nelson Mandela', Mateer writes: 'The poem is written in the form of a "praise-poem", inspired by the performances of Xhosa iimbongi. I wrote it after having ended a period of experiment in poetic form that had led to a kind of writing that I saw as excessively psychological and linguistic. This poem marked the start of my interest in the poem as "speech act" and poetry as a civic activity. "To Nelson Mandela" was intended for a performance at the Perth Institute of Contemporary Arts in 1996 and was part of a suite, others of which were addressed to the Aboriginal writer Mudrooroo and the notorious businessman Alan Bond'.

LES MURRAY. The poems which Murray hasn't discarded from the first 40-odd years of his career are gathered in his *Collected Poems 1961–2002* (Duffy & Snellgrove, 2002). Other books by the same author include *Fredy Neptune* (verse novel, 1998); *A Working Forest* (selected prose, 1997); and *The Full Dress* (poems matched with works in The National Gallery of Australia, 2001). He has won major prizes in Australia, Britain, and Germany, and his work has been published in seven European languages; further translations, into Hindi and Italian, are in progress.

Murray doesn't wish to comment on his poem 'Melbourne Pavement Coffee' except to say that the sports blazers mentioned in stanza three are those of Scotch College in Melbourne.

JAN OWEN is a South Australian poet whose fifth book *Timedancing* was published by Five Islands Press in December

2002. Awards for her work include the Mary Gilmore Prize, the Anne Elder Award, the Wesley Michel Wright Poetry Prize and the Gwen Harwood Poetry Prize. She has had residencies in Queensland, Tasmania, Rome, Malaysia and Paris where she spent six months in 2001 in the Nancy Keesing Studio at the Cité Internationale des Arts. In June 2002 she was a guest at the Maastricht International Poetry Nights. She is currently writing with the assistance of a two-year Fellowship from the Australia Council and her projects include poems based on Japanese wood-block prints, prose poems and fiction, parodies, and translations of Baudelaire's *Les Fleurs du Mal*.

Of 'The Pangolins', Owen writes: 'In 1997 I spent nine months in Malaysia, at Rimbun Dahan, the home of the Hijjas family set in a twelve-acre garden in a kampong twenty-seven kilometres out of Kuala Lumpur. One of my strongest impressions was a meeting, unexpectedly, at dusk, with a large wild animal. I couldn't make head nor tail of the creature at first and certainly had no name for it so there seemed no barrier of language or theory between us. I was touching the unknown, a gentle, benevolent-seeming presence, later understood to be the scaly anteater, *peng-goling* in Malaysian—"the roller". It was an intimate yet mysterious meeting, with other as self, which turned me away from my suddenly trivial human brooding. The memory is still vivid but largely wordless so this poem, written a couple of years later, is not about feeling; it's more a reflection on the patterns and synesthetic effect of a tropical night. The oddness of the animal-human encounter seemed humorously repeated the next day in the dogs' puzzlement at the safely rolled-up baby pangolin'.

LOUISE OXLEY was born in Hobart in 1955. She has taught English as a second language for many years, both in Australia and overseas. Her poems have appeared in a variety of Australian publications. Her first collection, *Compound Eye*, is due from Five Islands Press in 2003 as part of its New Poets Program.

Oxley writes: '"Voice Over" had its beginnings in a documentary on World War Two I was half-watching while doing the washing up late one evening. What caught my attention was the story of the sinking of a warship and the rescue, many days later, of survivors by a submarine crew. One of the men continued to tread water long after he was safe, and despite their best efforts, the crew could not make him stop. Years later these men were reliving the moment with great compassion and some bewilderment. I wrote a note in my notebook, but didn't come back to it for some time, when a first line arrived that seemed to have the right rhythm, and once I'd imagined myself into mountainous waves, the rest of the poem unfolded with unusual ease. The main concern of the poem is, I suppose, that despite the extraordinary capacity of the human species for tenderness, there is nothing, given both our own destructiveness and the power of natural forces, that can save us. This is probably a good thing'.

GEOFF PAGE has published 16 collections of poetry as well as two novels, a verse novel and several other works including anthologies, translations and a biography of the jazz musician, Bernie McGann. He retired at the end of 2001 from being in charge of the English Department at Narrabundah College in the ACT, a position he had held since 1974. He has won several awards, including the Queensland Premier's Literary Award for Poetry and the 2001 Patrick White Literary Award. His more recent books include: *The Scarring* (Hale & Iremonger, 1999); *Darker and Lighter* (Five Islands Press, 2001); *The Indigo Book of Modern Australian Sonnets* (editor) (Indigo, 2003); and *Drumming on Water* (Brandl & Schlesinger, 2003).

Of 'Five Poems from "A Good Wheat Paddock Spoiled"', Page writes: 'These poems are part of a longer sequence written from a close reading of the first issue of *The Canberra Times* (September 3, 1926). I find the distance between then and now rather poignant even though 1926 was only 14 years before I was born. I also think of all the great things that were going on elsewhere in the mid-twenties (Scott Fitzgerald's *The Great Gatsby*, for instance, or

Louis Armstrong's *Hot Five*) and realise just how bucolic the Canberra of that day must have been. And yet, as an increasingly satisfied Canberran since 1964, I still feel an affinity and a continuity with the Canberra of that period'.

VIVIENNE PLUMB was born in 1955 at the St George V. Memorial Hospital for Mothers and Babies in Camperdown, Sydney. Her mother was a New Zealander and her father an Australian. She has published a collection of short fiction, *The Wife Who Spoke Japanese In Her Sleep* (University of Otago Press, 1993), which was awarded the Hubert Church Prose Award (N.Z.), a novella, a playscript (awarded the Bruce Mason Award, N.Z.), and two collections of poetry, *Salamanca* (HeadworX, 1998), and *Avalanche* (Pemmican, 2000). Her novel, *Secret City*, is to be published during 2003. She held the Buddle Findlay Sargeson Fellowship in Auckland in 2001. She presently lives in Wellington, New Zealand.

Of 'Dry Riser Inlet', Plumb writes: 'I always liked the words, *dry riser inlet*. The letters and words you see around you in everyday circumstances often wield a strange power. I see "Dry Riser Inlet" as a dedication to the ones the *I Ching* refers to as the *small men*. For instance, *The way of small men appears to be increasing…the great are gone and the little come.* They think they run through the same landscape as you. They fancy they would like to be friends, in their longing to be the way they imagine you are. "Dry Riser Inlet" is also about love and yoga'.

PETER PORTER was born in Brisbane in 1929 and has been a resident in London since 1951. He has written more than twenty books of poetry, most recently *Collected Poems 1961–1999* (2 vols) (Oxford University Press) and *Max Is Missing* (Picador, 2001); and he edited *The Oxford Book of Modern Australian Verse* (1996). His honours include the Queen's Gold Medal for Poetry (2002) and the Forward Prize for Poetry (2002).

Of 'Komikaze', Porter writes: 'Suicide has always fascinated me. In my early twenties I wrote a Chekovian/Christopher Fry-like play, set on the Barrier Reef, in which Acts Two and Three ended in the main character's suicide attempts (successfully at the end)—title, *The Losing Chance*—happily never published. The Kamikaze pilots of World War Two were as brave as they were obsessional. I wanted to point up the comic absurdity of suicide: we are dead soon enough anyway. But I still find suicide heroic. More women attempt suicide than men. If you ascribe to a fundamental religion, most notably Christianity, then eternal punishment will stop your being extinguished totally. Grand funerals have their comic side: Saint-Simon, the toady of Louis Quatorze's Court, did suffer the ignomiy of his bowels (in a flask) exploding at his funeral. A horse being beaten sent Nietzsche mad in Turin: he had always deplored our cruelty to animals. In the penultimate stanza, I refer to the idea that perhaps primitive notions of torment by devils in Hell after death might be just the appropriate punishment for sophisticated people who have long since abandoned primitive religion. Final stanza: true story: the poet being buried was the Scottish Australian Alan Riddell and the man tossing the journal into the grave was Eddie Linden, editor of *Aquarius*; it was his latest issue'.

DAVID PRATER was born in Dubbo, New South Wales in 1972. He now lives in Melbourne from where he edits *Cordite Poetry Review*, an online magazine funded by the Australia Council. His poetry and prose have appeared in print and online journals including *Meanjin*, *Cordite*, *Going Down Swinging*, *Jacket*, *Slope* (USA), *JAAM* (NZ) and *Voiceworks*. Three of his poems were recently anthologised in *Short Fuse: A Global Anthology of Fusion Poetry* (Rattapallax, USA). David has performed his work at festivals (including Next Wave and The National Young Writers Festival), in various Melbourne venues and, most recently, in New York City. David's alter ego is Davey Dreamnation, a rock star with his own website: www.daveydreamnation.com.

David writes: "'Of a Dim Sim Nation" was based on a dream I had, in which my girlfriend (posing as some sort of snow bandit) rescued me from a dangerous arctic movie situation. The dream evoked such a strong feeling in me that I wrote the poem down almost as it appears now. It's essentially about protection, the need to feel safe in someone's arms. I think my girlfriend really loves this poem'.

PETER ROSE grew up in country Victoria and went to Monash University. Throughout the 1990s he was the Publisher at Oxford University Press in Australia. He is currently the Editor of *Australian Book Review*. He has published three books of poetry, most recently *Donatello in Wangaratta* (1998). In 2001 he published the award-winning family memoir, *Rose Boys*. His poetry, reviews, and journalism appear in various newspapers and magazines.

Rose writes: 'I find it hard to be prescriptive about my poems, especially one as allusive and elusive as "Late Edition". Suffice to say that I never—never—"get" a poem sitting at my desk. Poetry, for me, is not so much a vocation as a mood, a way of ruminating. My poems, however occluded, frequently touch on the epistemological divide, even between lovers. Here, the poet is sitting up late at night in the shadows of a cathedral, conceivably in Adelaide, reading Martin Amis's memoir *Experience*. A distant "sally of breaks" and rumoured collision remind him of the fragility of life and of the memoir he is himself trying to write, which deals with the profound emotional consequences of a similar road accident'.

DIPTI SARAVANAMUTTU was born in Sri Lanka, and came to Australia with her family at the age of eleven. From 1972 to 1994 she lived, or was based, in Sydney. She went to Killara High School and completed English Honours at Sydney University. Between third and fourth year at University she left study for a period of four years, during which time she worked as a journalist and reviewer for *Tribune* newspaper, and began publishing poetry, much influenced by both Australian postmodernism and the early poetry of Robert Gray, a strongly imagist poet. She also worked on the collective of a women's refuge (*Elsie's* had been started by Sydney University students in the seventies) and completed two filmscripts with a collective of women working on issues of racism and the migrant experience. She was a postgraduate student and teacher at the University of London around 1989–91. She has published two books of poetry and a novel, with another book of poems forthcoming in 2004.

Of 'Dingo Trails', Saravanamuttu writes: 'The poem was begun during a time when I was almost unable to write due to a combination of poverty and depression. Although completed almost seven years later, I have no idea why it manages to be funny. I think I was trying to write about my intellectual circumstances and the emotions surrounding them, given what for me were troubling times'.

MICHAEL SHARKEY was born in Sydney in 1946, and he first worked in publishing. He was educated at Sydney University and Auckland University, and has worked as an editor and book reviewer, and as a teacher in universities in Australia, New Zealand and China. He currently teaches Rhetoric, American Literature and English Composition at the University of New England in Armidale, NSW. His most recent publications are *Park* (Kardoorair, 2000), *Poems 2001* (Kardoorair, 2001) and *History: Selected Poems 1978–2000* (Five Islands Press).

Sharkey writes: 'Is it too easy to say that "Advantages of Daughters" was waiting to be written? There are many daughters in my extended family and, in adopting a father's point of view, I distilled years of familial and other lore. The theatre of family life is often comic. I extended the more-or-less unrhymed couplet frame that's something of a fallback with me. That mode lends itself to supple tonal shifts. It favours aphoristic tightness and the thought and speech rhythms that image the narrative and philosophic thrust of mindful conversation'.

R. A. SIMPSON was born in 1929. He was Poetry Editor of *The Age* from 1969 until 1997. In 1999, he won *The Age* Book of the Year for poetry with *The Impossible and Other Poems* (Five Islands Press).

He died in 2002. His collection *The Sky's Beach: Poems and Drawings* (Five Islands Press) will be published in 2003.

ALEX SKOVRON is the author of three collections of poetry: *The Rearrangement* (1988), *Sleeve Notes* (1992), and, most recently, *Infinite City* (1999), which was shortlisted in the *Age* Book of the Year and the Victorian Premier's Literary Awards. A fourth book, *The Man and the Map*, will appear in 2003. He has also published short stories, and a novella is forthcoming. A book editor since the early 1970s, he lives in Melbourne.

Of 'Once We Crossed the Equator', Skovron writes: 'This poem came to me while I was crossing Bass Strait aboard the old *Spirit of Tasmania*, in January 2002. I wrote it quite quickly, seated at a small table in one of the shipboard bar lounges. This context may account for, but can claim only a surface connection with, the poem's maritime atmosphere. It's a mysterious piece, a kind of rhetoric of passage at once unsettling and (I hope) beguiling. Each reader will no doubt interpret it differently'.

PETER SKRZYNECKI has published fourteen books of poetry and prose. He teaches at the University of Western Sydney. His prizes include the Grace Leven Poetry Prize and the Henry Lawson Short Story Award. His most recent book of poetry is *Time's Revenge* (2000). Other titles include *Immigrant Chronicle* (University of Queensland Press, 1975, 1992, 2002), which has been a set text on the New South Wales Higher School Certificate, and *Night Swim* (1989). His novels include *The Cry of the Goldfinch* (1986) and he has published two short story collections. He has also edited two collections of contemporary Australian fiction/poetry. In 1989 he received the Order of Cultural Merit from the Polish Government and in 2002 the Order of Australia (OAM) for his contribution to multicultural literature in Australia, particularly as a poet. University of Queensland Press will be publishing his memoir in 2004.

Of 'The Third Face in the Photograph', Skrzynecki writes: 'The story in the poem happened exactly as it's described. It was the last photograph taken with my mother before she died in which a third face—that of an Irish poet—was unintentionally included. Ironically, I met the poet two years later in Waterstones Bookshop, in Dawson Street, Dublin, at a poetry reading. When I read the poem and remember how the two incidents are related it spooks me…Who'd've thought it? The use of camera, film, etc, as metaphor should be self-explanatory. I suppose the poem is about kinship and mortality—about blood ties that exist even after death; it's also about whatever it is that binds poets together, the world over, in the name of poetry. It was written on 27 June 1999 in Sydney'.

NORMAN TALBOT came to Australia with Jean and their first child in 1963 and has lived in Newcastle, New South Wales, ever since. He has edited work by over 400 other people in over twenty collections and anthologies. He's had ten books and pamphlets of his own poetry published too, the first five books from the much lamented South Head Press, and the most recent a beautiful collaboration with the painter John Montefiore, *The Book of Changes* (John's painting there won the Sulman Award).

Of 'Resurrection at Cookham', Talbot writes: 'I'd seen "The Resurrection at Cookham" in England, in a Stanley Spencer exhibition, and loved his daggy, fleshly humans in their plodding defiance of the principle called conservation of mass as they experience physical resurrection. But I wouldn't have written about it, except that I attended a summer school run by Drew Lawson at the Quaker Yearly Meeting in Latrobe in 2001, and was issued with a postcard of it as a subject: Quakers like the juxtaposition of flesh and imagination. I couldn't get into it: a postcard isn't either an elephant or El Graco. So I wrote instead about Stanley painting it, talking to himself, celebrating both the factual death of the people he knew or felt he knew, and the spiritual outreach of impossible faith through the centuries of the country churchyard. I could reach something of him: the painter of flesh blinks most'.

JOHN TRANTER has lived at various times in Melbourne, Singapore, Brisbane and London, and he now lives in Sydney, where he is a company director. Sixteen collections of his verse have been published, including *The Floor of Heaven*, a book-length sequence of four verse narratives (HarperCollins, 1992 and Arc, 2001), *Late Night Radio* (Polygon, 1998), and *Heart Print* (Salt Publishing, 2001). In 1992 he edited (with Philip Mead) the *Penguin Book of Modern Australian Poetry*, a 470-page anthology which has become the standard text in its field, published in Britain and the USA as the *Bloodaxe Book of Modern Australian Poetry*. He is the editor of the free Internet magazine *Jacket*: www.jacketmagazine.com.

Of 'Brussels', Tranter writes: 'I spent six months as a writer-in-residence at Cambridge University in England in 2001 and 2002. For some reason, I found it difficult to write about my own experiences, and I ended up writing a sequence of loose "versions" of other poets' work, borrowing from Laforgue, Callimachus, Rilke, Baudelaire, Veronica Forrest-Thomson and others. The sequence was published as a pamphlet, titled "Borrowed Voices", by John Lucas's Shoestring Press in Nottingham. I have always respected Rimbaud's extraordinary talent. I chose this poem, "Brussels", partly because it is not one of his greatest or most important poems. It is almost an occasional piece, though the original has a hallucinatory quality I like'.

XUAN DUONG was born in Vietnam in 1945 and came to Australia 1978. He has written, in both English and Vietnamese, poetry, short stories and a cultural novel. Episodes of the novel entitled *The Tamarind Tree* have been published in issues of *Integration Magazine*, of which he is the founder. Currently he is working on a collection of poems entitled *WAR Pisses On My Dead Ancestor*, planned to be published in 2005 to mark thirty years since the end of the Vietnam War. His books of poems include: *Refugee Kosovo* (1999); *Refugee refugees see the East Timorese?* (2000); *Hey, I've got a racist flu!* (2002); and *Smiles on your river* (2003).

Of 'The July Rain', Xuan writes: 'Vietnam's monsoon rain becomes increasingly intense during July, rotting the soil. It washes away houses, drowns stock, people, fields. Rivers overflow and turn lands into rushing seas. The sky falls in, grey like inside a tunnel being sandblasted. The atmosphere induces tears which wrap around pain. All that is nowhere near the misery, fear, despair when one is being battered by the lashing rain, colluding with the beating wind, the tossing waves, and the falling sky full of touchable rolling rainy clouds. On that little wooden boat. In the rocking ocean. In the middle of the upside-down nowhere, the sky and the ocean exchange their places. Then the grey news photos of surviving Vietnamese asylum seekers being forcibly carried onto the aircraft and sent back enter the intense grey of monsoon rain atop that upside-down ocean. With the sky at the bottom'.

MARIA ZAJKOWSKI was born in Lower Hutt, New Zealand in 1973. She has lived in Australia for eight years and is currently located in Melbourne. Her work has appeared in literary journals in Australia and New Zealand as well as online. She received an Arts Victoria grant in 2001 to assist with her, as yet unpublished, collection of poems *From an Island*.

Zajkowski writes: 'When I wrote "The Grey Mare the Better Horse" I was someone else. There was suddenly so much space in my life to be this other person and in all that space I was alone. It was autumn, that spacious time of year. Obviously this other person was still me but it was me projected. Or perhaps it was me being aware of the possibility of projection which seemed to happen quite naturally. I hoped it was something like the feeling of autumn which is a natural thing yet all around there is the short-term satisfaction of daily human life. The poem is a recognition of time and the solitary nature of our own souls which are things, I think, forgotten far too often'.

JOURNALS WHERE THE POEMS WERE FIRST PUBLISHED

The Age, poetry ed. Gig Ryan. 250 Spencer Street, Melbourne, VIC 3000.

The Australian Book Review, ed. Peter Rose. PO Box 2320, Richmond South, VIC 3121.

Blue Dog: Australian Poetry, ed. Ron Pretty. c/o Poetry Australia. PO Box U34, Wollongong University, NSW 2500.

The Courier-Mail, book ed. Rosemary Sorensen. GPO Box 130, Brisbane, QLD 4001.

Famous Reporter, ed. Ralph Wessman. PO Box 368, North Hobart, TAS 7002.

Heat, poetry ed. Lucy Dougan. School of Language and Media. University of Newcastle, Callaghan, NSW 2308.

Island, acting poetry ed. Anthony Lawrence. PO Box 210, Sandy Bay, TAS 7006.

Meanjin, poetry ed. Peter Minter. 131 Barry Street, Carlton, VIC 3053.

Overland, poetry ed. John Leonard. PO Box 14146, Melbourne, VIC 8001.

papertiger: new world poetry, ed. Paul Hardacre. PO Box 5532, West End, QLD 4101.

Quadrant, literary ed. Les Murray. PO Box 82, Balmaine, NSW 2041.

Salt International Journal of Poetry and Poetics, ed. John Kinsella. Churchill College, University of Cambridge, England CB3 ODS.

Southerly, ed. Ian Britain. Department of English, Woolley Building A20, University of Sydney, NSW 2006.

The Sydney Morning Herald, acting literary ed. Malcolm Knox. GPO Box 506, Sydney, NSW 2001.

Westerly, eds. Delys Bird and Dennis Haskell. English, Communication and Cultural Studies, The University of Western Australia, Crawley, WA 6009.

ACKNOWLEDGMENTS

The general editors would like to thank Carol Hetherington for her research assistance with this book.

Grateful acknowledgment is made of the publications from which the poems in this volume were chosen.

Robert Adamson, 'Elegy'. *The Sydney Morning Herald* 4–5 May 2002, Spectrum: 13.

Jordie Albiston, 'Apostrophe'. *Island* 88 (2002): 75.

John Allison, 'Towards the Horizon'. *Meanjin* 1(2002): 44.

Judith Beveridge, 'Whisky Grass'. *Blue Dog: Australian Poetry* 1.1 (2002): 9.

Ken Bolton, 'A Prospect of the Young KB as a Critic'. *Heat* 4 NS (2002): 78–80. *Peter Boyle,* 'Nearness'. *Island* 89 (2002): 88–89.

Gary Catalano, 'Arles'. *The Age* 14 Dec. 2002, Saturday Extra: 9.

Jennifer Compton, 'Castle'. *Quadrant* 46.4 (2002): 78.

MTC Cronin, 'The Flower, The Thing'. *Heat* 3 NS (2002): 33.

Stephen Edgar, 'Eighth Heaven'. *Famous Reporter* 25 (2002): 118–19.

Michael Farrell, 'sydney'. *papertiger: new world poetry* 2 (2002).

Philip Hammial, 'Everlastingness'. *Southerly* 62.1 (2002): 178–79.

Jennifer Harrison, 'Funambulist'. *Blue Dog: Australian Poetry* 1.1 (2002): 32.

Mike Heald, 'Fire'. *Salt* 15 (2002): 102–03.

Clive James, 'Occupation: Housewife'. *Australian Book Review* June/July 2002: 29.

Judy Johnson, 'Self Pity'. *The Courier-Mail* 23 Feb. 2002.

Aileen Kelly, 'The Whirlpool'. *Blue Dog: Australian Poetry* 1.1 (2002): 41.

John Kinsella, 'Lyrical Unification in Gambier'. *Australian Book Review* Dec. 2001/Jan. 2002: 10.

Bronwyn Lea, 'These Gifts'. *Heat* 4 NS (2002): 146.

Geoffrey Lehmann, 'Father and Sons'. *Quadrant* 46.5 (2002): 58.

Emma Lew, 'The Clover Seed Hex'. *Island* 88 (2002): 50.

Jennifer Maiden, 'Missing Elvis'. *Southerly* 62.1 (2002): 21–24.

John Mateer, 'To Nelson Mandela'. *Overland* 168 (2002): 54–55.

Les Murray, 'Melbourne Pavement Coffee' *Quadrant* 46.12 (2002): 31.

Jan Owen, 'The Pangolins' *Quadrant* 46.12 (2002): 78.

Louise Oxley, 'Voice Over'. *Southerly* 62.1 (2002): 180.

Geoff Page, 'Five Poems from 'A Good Wheat Paddock Spoiled'. *Quadrant* 46.7–8 (2002): 70–71.

Vivienne Plumb, 'Dry Riser Inlet'. *Westerly* 47 (2002) 98–99.

Peter Porter, 'Komikaze'. *Australian Book Review* June/July 2002: 19.

David Prater, 'In a Dim Sea Nation'. *papertiger: new world poetry* 2 (2002).

Peter Rose, 'Late Edition'. *Meanjin* 1 (2002): 216.

Dipti Saravanamuttu, 'Dingo Trails'. 24 August 2002, Saturday Extra: 8.

Michael Sharkey, 'The Advantages of Daughters'. *Famous Reporter* 25 (2002): 40–42.

R. A. Simpson, 'Journeys Under the City'. *The Age* 27 July 2002, Saturday Extra: 8.

Alex Skovron, 'Once We Crossed the Equator'. *Salt* 15 (2002):234–35.

Peter Skrzynecki, 'The Third Face in the Photograph'. *Quadrant* 46.6 (2002): 37.

Norman Talbot, 'The Resurrection at Cookham'. *Heat* 4 NS (2002): 189–90.

John Tranter, 'Brussels'. *The Age* 31 Aug. 2002, Saturday Extra: 9.

Xuan Duong, 'The July Rain'. *Overland* 168 (2002): 20.

Maria Zajkowski, 'The Grey Mare the Better Horse'. *Heat* 4 NS (2002): 30.